WHAT PEOPLE ARE SAY!

AWAKENING CHILD

Heather Grace MacKenzie's wonderful book invites parents and those working with children to engage in a journey of self-acceptance and self-compassion in order to create a more peaceful life, both for ourselves and for our children. We come to realise that the best way to learn something is to teach it. Her words reflect her deep understanding of the subject-matter and, as always, come from the heart.
Lorraine Murray, author of *Calm Kids: Help Children Relax with Mindful Activities*

The insightful advice included in your book is in high demand at the moment, and the addition of your own experiences with your sons and from your teaching that you use to support the advice makes it all the more powerful and convincing. This combination works well, and I am sure there is a large audience for a book such as yours on mindfulness, especially with regard to parenting, at present.
Claire Gillman, Book Report for *Writers' Workshop*

Awakening Child

A journey of inner transformation through
teaching your child mindfulness
and compassion

Awakening Child

A journey of inner transformation through
teaching your child mindfulness
and compassion

Heather Grace MacKenzie

BOOKS

Winchester, UK
Washington, USA

First published by O-Books, 2016
O-Books is an imprint of John Hunt Publishing Ltd., Laurel House, Station Approach,
Alresford, Hants, SO24 9JH, UK
office1@jhpbooks.net
www.johnhuntpublishing.com

For distributor details and how to order please visit the 'Ordering' section on our website.

Text copyright: Heather Grace MacKenzie 2015

ISBN: 978 1 78535 408 3
Library of Congress Control Number: 2016931750

A CIP catalogue record for this book is available from the British Library.

Design: Stuart Davies

Printed and bound by CPI Group (UK) Ltd, Croydon, CR0 4YY, UK

We operate a distinctive and ethical publishing philosophy in all
areas of our business, from our global network of authors to
production and worldwide distribution.

CONTENTS

Preface 1

1. Introduction 2
2. Background 8
3. Connectedness – whispers of the heart 14
   3.1 Exercise: Holding Space for Ourselves
   – Heart Cave* 17
4. Awakening Child 24
   Aware 26
   4.1 Exercise: Breath Awareness* 26
   Compassionate 30
   4.2 Exercise: Self-Compassionate Intention* 33
   Embodied 36
   4.3 Exercise: Sensing Mode* 36
   4.4 Exercise: Body Scan* 38
5. Understanding Stress 47
   Children and Stress 53
6. Mindfulness, Meditation, Visualisation and Insight 57
   The origins of mindfulness 58
   6.1 Exercise: Exploring Meditation Together 62
   6.2 Exercise: Shower of Light Visualisation* 64
7. Benefits of Meditation 70
   What does the available research show? 71
8. Method – the 'How' 75
   8.1 Exercise: Purple Feathers 76
   Environment 77
   Posture 78
   Intention and Motivation – what's important to you? 80
   8.2 Exercise: Make a Snow Globe 82
   Grounding 85
   Support – Mindfulness of Breath 87
   8.3 Exercise: Heart Breathing 88

	Alternative Support – Mindfulness of Sound	88
	8.4 Exercise: Sound Awareness*	89
	When to Practise and How Long	93
	Sustaining Practice	94
9.	Attitude – the 'What'	97
	Guiding Light 1: Beginner's Mind	98
	Guiding Light 2: Non-striving	99
	Guiding Light 3: Non-judging	100
	Guiding Light 4: Patience	101
	Guiding Light 5: Trust	101
	Guiding Light 6: Acceptance	102
	Guiding Light 7: Letting Go	103
	Playfulness	107
	Wonder	107
	Limitlessness	108
	Flow	108
	Connection	109
	Cycles	109
	Delivering our Gifts	110
10.	Taming the Amygdala	112
	Mindfulness of Touch	113
	10.1 Exercise: Gentle Touch	113
	Relaxing Visualisation	115
	10.2 Exercise: The Waterfall*	116
	Soothing Words	118
	10.3 Exercise: Soothing Words*	118
	Progressive Muscle Relaxation	120
	10.4 Exercise: Tensing and Softening	120
11.	Mindfulness in Daily Life	124
	11.1 Exercise: Mindful Malteser-Eating	126
12.	Let the Magic Live On	132
	12.1 Exercise: Fairy Door*	134
13.	The Wisdom of the Body	139
	Mindful Movement	142

13.1 Exercise: Mindful Walking*   143

13.2 Exercise: Body and Mind Letters   146

Reflection   147

14. A Balancing Act   149

15. Tips for Leading Meditations   154

16. Meditations for Younger Children   161

16.1 Parent and Child Exercise: Eskimo Kisses   162

16.2 Exercise: Tracing the Flower   163

16.3 Exercise: Finding the Perfection   164

16.4 Exercise: Where's my Body?   165

Further ideas for younger children   168

17. Meditations for Teens   171

17.1 Exercise: MOP (Moment of Presence)   173

17.2 Exercise: MOK (Moment of Kindness)   174

17.3 Exercise: Bodykind   175

Additional exercises for teens   179

Not interested?   180

18. At the Heart of it All – BE.LOVE   182

18.1 Exercise: Inner Child Healing*   183

19. Working with Groups   193

Practicalities and Holding Space   196

Environment   197

Motivation   198

Flexibility   199

Relating to the Group Members   200

Embodiment of mindfulness   200

Guiding group practices   201

Inquiry   201

Creating a Compassionate Classroom   204

20. In Awe and Wonder – a final message   207

20.1 Exercise: A Final Reflection   208

Appendix A – Resources for Adults   210

Appendix B – Resources for Children   213

Acknowledgements

My circle of allies: my children, stepchildren and my beloved, my departed loved ones (grandparents, parents), the Mindfulness Association (including, in particular, Rob Nairn, Heather Regan-Addis, Fay Adams and Choden), those who've lifted me and taught me to fly (Lorraine Murray, Amy Palko, Kathleen Prophet, Annu Tara, Peggy Dylan, Stephen Mulhearn, Oona McFarlane), my friends and those who've chosen to learn with me. In particular I would like to thank Rachael Young for her unfailing belief that this book would reach the bookshelves and find its way to the hearts of those who need it. Deepest gratitude to those who have provided ceaseless support, love, and held a desire to co-create a world that's a better place for our children.

Preface

The most precious gift we can offer anyone is our attention. When mindfulness embraces those we love, they will bloom like flowers.
Thich Nhat Hanh

All parents know that parenting is the toughest job in the world – we're on duty twenty-four hours a day, looking after the mental, emotional, physical and spiritual health of our child. It almost feels like a part of us is living outside of our body, and the unconditional love that we feel for our child can render us very vulnerable and potentially very fearful. We often feel like we're getting this parenting thing horribly wrong and beat ourselves up for our parenting 'failures' almost incessantly. We worry that we are failing to instil in our child the necessary skills to enable them to live happy and fulfilling lives. We can be riddled with self-doubt and 'what if?' questions.

An argument could be made that the job of a school teacher or social worker comes a close second, in terms of the level of difficulty, to the 'job' of being a parent! Whilst this book is predominantly written for parents, there is much within the following pages that will be very relevant for those working with children. So whether you're a parent, a teacher, social worker, counsellor or work with children in some other capacity, it is my sincere hope that this book will inspire and motivate you as well as give you some very practical ideas for bringing mindfulness into your relationship with your child or children that you work with, and for teaching children the power of mindfulness and visualisation.

1

Introduction

There is a special place in life,
that needs my humble skill,
A certain job I'm meant to do,
which no one else can fulfil.

The time will be demanding,
and the pay is not too good
And yet I wouldn't change it
for a moment – even if I could.

There is a special place in life,
a goal I must attain,
A dream that I must follow,
because I won't be back again.

There is a mark that I must leave,
however small it seems to be,
A legacy of love for those
who follow after me.

There is a special place in life,
that only I may share,
A little path that bears my name,
awaiting me somewhere.

There is a hand that I must hold,
a word that I must say,
A smile that I must give
for there are tears to blow away.

There is a special place in life
that I was meant to fill
A sunny spot where flowers grow,
upon a windy hill.

There's always a tomorrow
and the best is yet to be,
And somewhere in this world,
I know there is a place for me.
Anonymous

I watch him quietly, this little miracle of creation. He's sleeping now; his boisterous energy has come to rest. The soft glow of the lamp illuminates his perfect alabaster skin and slightly flushed cheeks. Little freckles dot his cheeks and nose, his chest gently rises and falls and a small sigh escapes from his lips. He's wearing his favourite light-blue farm-vehicle pyjamas; they're mostly covered by his bed covers, but a little foot peeks out from beneath. As I reach out to touch his silky blonde hair, he stirs and moves his head to snuggle his cheek into my hand. A glimmer of a smile plays across his face as if he knows mummy's here, and I know that on some level he's aware that I'm close by. I witness each beautiful moment unfolding, aware of the flow of my own breath, feeling the cool air rush past the insides of my nostrils, the expansion of the chest, the stretching sensations in the muscles of the abdomen, the pause, the softening of the belly, the fall of the chest, the warmer air rushing past the insides of the nostrils on the out-breath. I'm aware of the sensations of pressure and contact between the soles of my feet and the soft carpet fibres, and tiny adjustments that my muscles make to keep my body balanced. The faint awareness of my pulse, the beating of my heart, underlying each moment. Using *all* of my senses enables me to inhabit the moment as fully as I can.

Being Logan's mother for the past six years has been one of

the greatest gifts of my life, along with mothering his two older brothers, Connor (aged fifteen) and Ethan (aged thirteen). Each of my children shows me, in each moment that I'm present, whether my communication is clear, whether they feel heard and therefore respected, and whether I'm present to their needs and also my own. Meditation, and in particular the practice of mindfulness meditation, brings us to this place of presence, where it is possible to connect in each moment to a feeling of aliveness in every cell of the body, tapping into a deep ocean of stillness and wisdom within and a heartfelt sense of the common humanity that links us all. This doesn't mean that we are always in a zen state of complete equanimity – far from it! But the possibility is always there, that in any moment of conflict we can choose a different path – the path of present-moment awareness, which allows us to respond more skilfully to what's going on.

My intention with this book is to offer what is perhaps a slightly different way of interacting with your child or children that you work with, indeed a different way of being. I shall introduce the principles of mindfulness first of all to set the scene a little, and then we can explore the journey of bringing those principles into a lived reality that can enhance the quality of your relationship with your child (and others) in a fairly extraordinary way. I will then share some of my experience of authentic ways to share mindfulness with children, including tips for working with different age groups.

Whilst I very much recognise the value of visualisation, both in terms of its power to relax and also help us to get in touch with the energies of the heart, this is primarily a book aimed at fostering mindful parenting and self-compassion through teaching your child mindfulness. Whilst we touch in on some ideas for relaxing visualisations – and these are particularly useful at bedtime or for calming an anxious child – this book is perhaps not for you if you hope that after reading and digesting it you will become accomplished in delivering guided journey meditations to your child; the emphasis here will be on learning to *lean in* to the present moment and soften around any difficulties we experience, whilst bringing in our creativity to capture our child's imagination.

Now would be a perfect moment to say that I'm most certainly not a perfect parent, nor do I have all the answers! My children are not always full of joy, perfectly confident, perfectly content, perfectly at ease. This is OK! In fact, it's *more* than OK – it's in perfect alignment with this oftentimes messy thing we call 'life'. It's taken quite a bit of time, but I've got much better at letting go of striving for perfection. I remember when I was a child, around 11 years old, rushing to tell my grandmother that I'd got ninety-eight per cent in a maths exam, expecting her face to break into a broad smile and for praise to come my way, but instead she looked at me quite seriously and said, "What happened to the other two per cent?" I can look back at that moment now with humour and also sensitivity for the upbringing my grandmother must have had, but at the time it sent a pretty powerful message to me that nothing less than perfection is good enough. But if throughout our lives we're always striving for perfection then we're going to be spending pretty much all of our time in a state of disappointment and self-criticism! There is a famous adage, "Pain is inevitable; suffering is optional." My goodness, we're good at heaping suffering on to ourselves, with a harsh self-critic often giving a running commentary on our failings and an underlying sense of not quite being good enough in some way; mindfulness (and the other wing of the bird – compassion) really help us to explore our attitude towards our inner and outer landscapes with curiosity and kindness, and can give us a zoomed-out perspective of the futility and unhelpfulness of many of our underlying beliefs and much of our behaviour.

Given the explosion of interest in mindfulness, there are now a great many books available that aim to teach the reader mindfulness and compassion and they do it very well; I've recommended some that I've found particularly helpful in Appendix A – Resources for Adults. However, no book can do full justice to the power of mindfulness and the journey of culti-vating it and teaching it. You may well already have some experience of mindfulness, and if not then this book will give you an introduction to the subject, but it is impossible to teach mindfulness to a child, or indeed anyone, without practising mindfulness ourselves – simply reading about it is not enough. Mindfulness is essentially a different way of living, and so it's really helpful to practise daily so that the seeds of mindfulness can really take root and flourish. There are practices suitable for adults scattered throughout this book, so that you can get started on your mindfulness journey right away if you haven't already, but learning in a group setting with a properly trained mindfulness teacher is to be highly recommended in order to navigate the pitfalls when getting started. If you haven't already attended an 8-week mindfulness course such as Mindfulness-Based Stress Reduction (MBSR), Mindfulness-Based Cognitive Therapy (MBCT), Mindfulness Association Mindfulness Based Living Course (MBLC), Mindful Self-Compassion (MSC) or similar, then I humbly suggest that you take the plunge and enrol in a local course, or enrol in an online 'live teaching' course if there isn't a course in your local area. There is a list of resources in Appendix A to help you find a course. To teach mindfulness we must embody mindfulness in our daily lives, else we are well meaning but inauthentic. Children can sniff the unpleasant whiff of, "Do as I say, not what I do" a mile off!

For ease of reference throughout the book, I will refer to a child or young person that you're working with as 'your child'. Most of the techniques suggested can be easily adapted for groups of children (two or more) either at home, at school, holiday club etc., but I'll address issues specifically related to teaching mindfulness to groups of children in Chapter 19.

It is my hope that this book will help you to:

- learn more about mindfulness and how to lead a child (or children) in simple mindfulness practices,
- create a calmer, more harmonious household,
- support your child in fulfilling their incredible potential,
- help your child to learn to deal with strong emotions such as anger, disappointment etc.,
- develop a daily mindfulness practice for yourself that feels both nurturing and sustainable,
- learn greater self-compassion (which then naturally flows to your child and helps them to learn it),
- come to see the power in allowing and expressing vulnerability, and
- realise the power of embodiment – when we embody mindfulness then the teaching takes care of itself.

If you wish to nurture a child or children, to help them move through life with as much ease as possible, to live in expression of their fullest potential and to feel respected, supported and nurtured, then you are making a difference already through that intention. You are connecting with your own highest potential and creating a more peaceful and harmonious future for us all. Thank you!

2

Background

Twelve years ago I was a software engineer heading up the Support Team at a small but rapidly growing IT company in Edinburgh. I wasn't very sociable, preferring the company of computers and animals to humans, having had a fairly difficult and relatively solitary upbringing by my mother on a windy Scottish island. My job was high-pressured and I was often bothered with minor health complaints. Connor and Ethan were aged three and one respectively, and like all working mothers I really struggled to balance my working life with being the best mother that I could be. Then one cold winter evening in 2003 everything changed. My husband told me that he'd been having an affair. My emotional life until then had been extremely unremarkable; I had in many ways been living my life on autopilot, thinking that I was just quite emotionally well-balanced but in retrospect I had actually been rather emotionally closed-down. Suddenly I was consumed by so many difficult-to-deal-with emotions: anger, rage, despair, sadness, fear, shame, jealousy, confusion and much more. Physically I felt deeply ill; it felt as if these new emotions had joined forces with those that had been locked down deep inside me since early childhood and this dark stuff felt quite unbearable – it was simply overwhelming, and felt as if it was literally choking the life out of me.

Connor and Ethan were so very little when their father moved out. Having experienced growing up without a father, I desperately didn't want my children to grow up without a father in their lives, yet history seemed in a certain way to be repeating itself. My mother was a very spiritual woman, certain that everything happens for a reason, but deep down she was lost when my father died. A part of her died with him, and she spent much of her remaining life using alcohol to numb the pain. I often wonder how different life might have been for me and my sister if she had learned mindfulness and found a way to relate differently to the pain that was eating her up inside.

In 2004, in the midst of divorce proceedings, I attended a Reiki First Degree workshop with a wonderful lady called Lorraine Urquhart (now Lorraine Murray), with absolutely no idea why I was there or what I'd be learning, but with a quiet and slightly confusing sense that somehow I was *supposed* to be there. We did some meditation that day and one of the visualisations took us to a safe place where a compassionate being appeared to us. I visualised my father, who had passed away when I was four years old, waiting for me in a small log cabin with a fire burning. We had a conversation that I don't remember, but I do remember the soft look of unconditional love on his face, and that image will remain with me always. That was my first experience of compassionate imagery, and it was so powerful that I sobbed for the best part of an hour. It felt as if something shifted in me that day and I knew that somehow I had stumbled on to the right path (a process I now recognise as listening to my intuition) but there was much work to be done – I had to learn to be with the incredibly difficult emotions that still flooded my body and I had to find a way to help my mind and body move back towards balance.

Lorraine taught me to imagine surrounding difficult people and situations with a loving pink light – pink being one of the colours of the heart energy centre. I practised this over and over again, initially focusing on my husband and quickly realising that my striving nature had led me to commence in a rather unhelpful place – the task just seemed too enormous! I carried on practising with those I was having minor difficulties with or with people I didn't even know – for example, noticing a couple arguing outside a local shop or seeing a young child crying at the zoo. Looking back, this heralded the start of my willingness to approach suffering and take action, the start of my cultivation of compassion. My personality had started to change quite dramatically after a year or so of these practices. I had gone from being a very 'left-brained' software engineer, liking my world to be defined by logic and reason, to being much more creative, much more in touch with my emotions and my intuition, and much more loving! After a year or so, in spite of going ahead with divorce proceedings, my soon-to-be-ex-husband was one of my best friends and I had changed careers, leaving my very well-paid software engineering job for the much less well-paid job of health-shop owner.

Although my childhood often felt incredibly difficult and as a teenager I was extremely shy and introverted, I now count my childhood and the breakdown of my marriage as some of the greatest blessings in my life because I believe that those difficulties have caused me to grow and to seek a different way of being; difficulties sometimes have a way of making life so uncomfortable that we have almost no choice but to seek an alternative way of relating to our experience. My difficulties have caused me to seek to understand my place in the world. Perhaps you have also experienced this sense of difficulty causing you to seek a different way? Maybe that's why you have come to read this book; perhaps you've experienced some challenges in parenting that have caused you to seek a more enlightened way of being with your child, one that does not revolve around conflict and battles of will?

Happily, it is not necessary to find the path of present-moment living via difficulty; we can choose to lead children towards this path right from birth! In fact, children are already very good at living in the present moment from the moment they are born, experiencing each moment from a sensory perspective rather than a thinking perspective. How quickly as children we learn that logical, rational *thinking mode* is much more valued in our society than *sensing mode*, and what a tragedy this is! Before we know it we start to feel like heads rushing through space, seeing our bodies (when we occasionally choose to think about them) as slightly inconvenient vehicles that carry our heads around – our bodies don't look as we might wish, don't behave entirely as we would like, and regularly (sometimes rather inconveniently) need to be refuelled. And yet *the body is the doorway to all that we seek*. A bold statement, I know, and I hope to justify that statement in the remaining pages of this book.

I continued to learn Reiki with Lorraine until completing my training as a Reiki Master Teacher in 2010. I have been teaching different forms of meditation, including some underpinning themes of mindfulness such as loving-kindness, since that time and it has been an incredibly rewarding journey. I have been teaching my own children meditation for many years, and since 2012, as a Professional Level tutor of Lorraine's amazing Connected Kids™ programme, I've been teaching meditation and mindful activities to children in a professional capacity. Some of my experiences with children in these meditation sessions are what have motivated me to want to look more closely at the benefits that meditation can offer children. After just a couple of sessions with me, an 8-year-old boy whose father had passed away two years previously volunteered to start sleeping in his own bed again. He hadn't done that since his father's passing. I started to look into what research was available to present to parents and head teachers to support the value of teaching children meditation, and the word 'mindfulness' seemed to be everywhere.

I searched for more information on the definition of mindfulness and its related themes and discovered many links on the Internet to information regarding Mindfulness-Based Stress Reduction (MBSR) training. I read more about the 8-week course and decided to attend an MBSR course run by one of the Mindfulness Association tutors, Chloe Homewood-Allen, in 2012. Watching the change in the other participants on the course, many of whom were attending with significant anxiety and stress-related illnesses, was quite inspirational, and I was struck by Chloe's embodiment of acceptance and allowing. Those who initially appeared quite pale, nervy and unsmiling after a few weeks on the course started to have more colour in their cheeks and a noticeably warmer and more relaxed demeanour. Chloe guided us to recognise that there was nothing wrong with us and we didn't need to be 'fixed', that we are intrinsically whole and that this is fundamental to our nature as human beings. The idea of 'not needing to be fixed' was quite a revelation to me and my problem-solving brain! I was starting to see why mindfulness as a way of life could quite radically change people's lives for the better and how the secular manner in which it is taught really makes it accessible to everyone. I was hooked, and wanted to understand more and be able to share this with others. I now find myself with a Postgraduate Diploma in Studies in Mindfulness and studying for a PhD in Education with Aberdeen University that includes creating and evaluating a course in mindfulness and self-compassion for secondary school pupils, on behalf of the Mindfulness Association. How life changes in a few short years!

The modern-day danger of sanitising mindfulness and completely extracting it from its Buddhist origins is that we lose the wider context; we lose some of the essential essence of what mindfulness points to which is our spiritual nature (Buddhists call this our 'Buddha nature') – the core of who we are that is beyond our current physical form. One of the greatest gifts we can give our children is an awareness of their inner light that transcends their current energy footprint (which we may term their 'personality'). Learning Reiki, and therefore bringing my energy more into balance, has changed my personality immeasurably and it has become apparent to me through direct experience that our behaviour only reflects our current energy footprint, or personality. Who we are is most definitely not who we think we are; indeed, who we truly are is quite beyond the limits of thought. When we recognise this, it then becomes so much easier not to blame someone for their behaviour or to hold grudges because we realise that the behaviour is only a reflection of the state of the person's energy in that moment and that energy is very often quite out-of-balance. We can teach a child how to bring their energy more into balance through practising mindfulness and visualisation, and in doing so our own energy will become more balanced. The layers of habitual patterns and unhelpful beliefs that shroud us in darkness start to fall away and our inner light starts to shine so much more brightly.

3

Connectedness – whispers of the heart

Throughout our lives we long to love ourselves more deeply and to feel connected with others. Instead, we often contract, fear intimacy, and suffer a bewildering sense of separation. We crave love, and yet we are lonely. Our delusion of being separate from one another, of being apart from all that is around us, gives rise to all of this pain.
Sharon Salzberg

Cultivation of the more loving side of my nature, along with the deep curiosity around the mysteries of life that often accompanies those of us born with a sun sign of Scorpio, led me down a spiritual path that was always going to be quite avoidant of religion, having had a strict boarding-school upbringing where church-going was forced upon us. I grew up in a household of pick-and-mix spirituality – my mother believed in an all-powerful being that she called 'God' and yet she also believed in reincarnation. Our local minister told my mother that even though she believed in God she would surely go to hell as she didn't attend the local church on a weekly basis. As a teenager this was more than enough proof for me that religion (and I generalised here to include *all* religions) was very deeply misguided! I knew in my heart, indeed in every cell of my body, that whatever power had brought us into being was all-loving and non-judging. The Internet has facilitated a monumental shift in bringing the power to the people rather than to religious institutions. Knowledge is power, and until the advent of the Internet much knowledge was confined within institutions and books. So many avenues of belief are now open to us, and we can now share experiences with each other at the touch of a button. Religious dogma can now easily be questioned – opened up to exploration amongst the worldwide 'community'. We can see that in essence all faiths point to the same deep truths, but the human mind has the capability of misinterpreting teachings to suit its own beliefs and its own agendas.

Although I follow no particular religion, Reiki (and compassion practices associated with it) brought me over and over again to the notion of spiritual 'awakening' and I had a sense that deep down a part of me knew what this meant, even if my conscious mind didn't know. I eventually came across *A Course in Miracles* and, despite the intensely Christian language, several teachers in my life helped me to decipher and distil the message of awakening until I finally understood that what I have believed in, all of my life, without truly realising it, is oneness. Ironically, given my great mistrust of religion in general as a teenager, I then realised that this is the seed of wisdom that all religions point to.

A Course in Miracles teaches that in each moment of difficulty, each moment of conflict, each moment of suffering, we can always open our hearts and accept the miracle – a shift in perception – and this shift in perception is one that moves us closer to our true nature through the very act of opening the heart. As we learn to *open the heart, in spite of our deepest fears* that this may allow others to trample on it, somehow it seems that this is a leap of faith that we must take in order to fully open to our incredible potential as human beings.

As I often say to students, "Each time we open our mouths to lead a child in a meditation, we stand at the edge of a cliff and jump, trusting that the ground will rise up to meet us." For we lead the meditation from the heart, we are there with the child, experiencing the practice ourselves, and we don't know how the practice will be received. Particularly with my own children, my greatest fear was that they might laugh or poke fun at my sometimes clunky (certainly in my first forays into trying to lead meditations) but always tender-hearted words, and this was in essence a fear of rejection! Yet the more we practise, the more we realise that as long as we lead a meditation from the heart and let go of expectations then whatever follows is just rather perfect – both the adult and child will receive whatever lessons are meant to be received; there's a kind of divine order to what transpires – a kind of magic – when we listen to the whispers of the heart.

My compassion practices had always been aimed towards others, and yet I was aware that I healed as I practised. It started to dawn on me that perhaps separation is an illusion; that we're all actors in one grand play in the mind of one single being. Perhaps there is no 'me' or 'I' and this idea of self is just an illusion. This may be too far-out a concept for many, and yet I invite you, as you practise the exercises in this book, to observe what happens to you and to those around you. When we work on ourselves, we find that the benefits ripple outwards and others mirror the changes happening inside us, and so perhaps this in itself is proof of the interconnectedness of all things. Holding in our hearts and minds the interconnected nature of all things is a wonderful antidote to the egocentricity that is very much part of Western culture where everything revolves around *me* – what *I* like and what *I* don't like.

The process of teaching mindfulness to a child is essentially working with the fabric of our hearts and a vehicle for our own healing and transformation. As children, we seek and blossom in unconditional love, but, being parented by the wounded, we rarely receive it. Love, yes, but not unconditional love where we truly feel that *every* aspect of us is accepted and cherished. We learn to hide the less acceptable parts of ourselves, the jealous thoughts, the resentful thoughts, the uncharitable thoughts, because more love seems to come if we present ourselves as happy, amenable, sociable, 'nice'. We come to the (misguided) perception that we are only loveable if we express wholesome, positive emotions; we learn what our parents and our peers value and, consciously or unconsciously, present those aspects of ourselves that fit with those values and try to hide those parts of ourselves that don't. The aspects of us that don't fit with our view of what is acceptable – the darker parts of ourselves, or 'shadow self' – can only be healed and transformed when we shine the light of acceptance on them... this is the inner work of teaching a child meditation – we heal ourselves, including our inner child, as we do.

Even as I continue to write this book, I've become more aware of the inner processes that drive me as I write, perhaps Mother's Day bringing into my awareness the realisation that maybe the way I've been writing is directed in some way in pleasing my mother, although she's no longer here. That awareness sets me free, and I realise that I've been feeling a little constrained in my writing simply because there's been a subtle sense of wanting Mum to be proud of what I'm writing. There's perhaps even an image in my mind of her editing my work as I write, and she could certainly be quite critical! It's time to let go of that now and just let the words arrive from the heart, for it has a wisdom all of its own if I can get my head out of the way. Some of the writing may not always make complete logical sense therefore – words are such limited pointers to a much deeper truth – but it is my deepest wish that the words may in some way be helpful and indeed that something more fundamental and timeless beneath the words may touch your heart.

I think it's reasonable for me to assume that you're hoping for change in your life in relation to your interactions with a child, given that you're reading this book. In which case, now is probably a great moment to share one of the biggest nuggets of wisdom that my teachers have shared with me at different times in my life: it is absolutely imperative that we learn to direct an authentic kindness towards ourselves in times of difficulty – this is how we build our inner reservoir of strength with which to face those parts of us that need our tender attention in order to heal. On the journey of reading this book, I humbly ask that you intend to hold a space for yourself that is uncritical, tender, gentle and nurturing. This is alien to many of us – it certainly was to me – but by growing your self-compassion, you will be building your inner resources to begin to look more honestly at the habitual patterns and unresolved conditioning that cause you to react in certain ways, and by growing your ability to stay present you will start to create the space around triggering events that will enable you to respond much more skilfully to the demands of the situation rather than react unconsciously. Here is an exercise that will help you to set that intention. You may wish to find a place where you are unlikely to be disturbed as you go through each practice, and as with all of the practices in this book it will perhaps help to have a journal with you so that you can flow-write after the exercise (it's a wonderful excuse, if you need one, to buy new stationery!).

I have numbered each practice for ease of reference, with the first part of the number referring to the chapter in which it appears and the second part of the number referring to the number of the practice within the chapter. Practices with an asterisk (*) suffix are available as more detailed recorded meditations at www.heathergrace.co.uk/AwakeningChildPractices. As you're reading any practice in this book, you may find it helpful to treat the reading of the exercise as an actual meditation, setting the intention to be as fully present as possible and maybe even imagining that you're breathing in the words as you read. Between each paragraph, take the time to pause and see if you can allow yourself to take a couple of full and renewing breaths before moving on to the next paragraph. This will help the mind to move into a more experiential state, and more of a state of intuitive *being* rather than active, logical *doing*. As with all of the practices set out in this book, each and every time you notice your mind has wandered off into thinking, simply bring it back to the present moment by refocusing your attention on the guidance given, and the words you see in front of you.

3.1 Exercise: Holding Space for Ourselves – Heart Cave*

Find a place to practise where you're unlikely to be disturbed and please let go of any guilt in relation to taking time for you – it is not selfish, it is skilful. Taking time for you is absolutely essential – think of it like putting on your oxygen mask first; you can't help those around you if you've passed out through lack of oxygen! As part of taking time for you and making this time special, you may wish to light a candle, or place some objects of significance in the space around you.

Find a posture in which to sit or lie that reflects the importance of giving yourself space, and begin to find the place in your body where you are most aware of your breath. Noticing your breath in a light way and not trying to change it, just observing its flow.

Maybe saying to yourself in your mind's eye as you breathe in, "Breathing in, I know I'm breathing in..." and on the out-breath saying to yourself, "Breathing out, I know I'm breathing out," just for a few breaths.

Taking your attention now to the body as a whole, as it rests here. What's going on for your body right now? Allowing the body to present sensations for you to notice. Perhaps there are areas of the body that are in contact with something and experiencing sensations of contact and pressure. What does that feel like?

Maybe there are tingles or glows, aches or niggles, warm bits or cold bits? Spending some time with the sensations of the body, as they present themselves in each moment, with a sense of tending kindly (as best you can) to whatever arises.

And now bringing to mind a place that feels really nurturing. No rush to bring this place to mind, just setting the intention to visualise or have a felt sense of being in a place that feels safe, non-judging, gentle and deeply nurturing. A place that accepts you exactly as you are. It could be a real place that you've been to, or an imaginary place, or a mixture of the two, but it's a place that has all of the qualities of safety and care, and a place that actually rejoices in you being there. Maybe it's an outdoor place – a beach that you've visited, or a garden, forest or lake. Perhaps it's an indoor place that feels like your sanctuary.

Spending some time seeing if you can fill in some of the details of this place in your mind's eye; either visualising or having a felt sense of the beauty of this place, the feeling of this place, the textures, the sounds.

And in this place, seeing if it's possible to open to thoughts, emotions and physical sensations with curiosity and kindness, even if they don't feel particularly pleasant. Setting the intention to bring a warmth and care to whatever arises and allowing this place to support you unconditionally as you rest here for as long as you need.

I remember attending one of the first Connected Kids Level 1 courses in 2011, convinced of the benefits of meditation through my own experience of it and teaching it to adults, and keen to try some techniques with my own children. I was utterly terrified by the prospect of delivering a meditation to one of my children and having them 'reject' me in some way, either laughing at my complete incompetence or being completely bored and disinterested in something that was quite important to me. I was aware of the fear, and like so many other fears in my life, very curious about it and determined to approach it with curiosity rather than run away from it.

My relationship with my two eldest children, who were still of primary school age at the time, was full of resistance. I attempted to coerce my children into the behaviour that I wanted, parenting them as I had been parented myself. Somehow I had become a carbon copy of my own mother in spite of my own best efforts. My attempts at controlling my children (threats, naughty step, rewarding good behaviour and punishing the 'bad' by removing privileges) were met sometimes with unwilling compliance, and often with outright rebellion! My journey of teaching meditation to my children has been a journey of self-discovery indeed… learning that we are being taught just as much as we are teaching, learning that our need for control usually comes from our fears, and learning to let go, one at a time, of the habitual patterns of parenting that I had so unconsciously been exhibiting.

My children reflected back to me each of my beliefs about myself, and their resistance to me reflected my own inner resistance, frustration and resentment. Teaching my children meditation became a joyful process of trial-and-error and empowering my children to make choices – to learn in a safe way to skilfully navigate their way through life. It was starting to become so clear that the time we spent together deliberately cultivating a *softer* way of being together was transforming our relationship. Together, we started to explore our feelings with curiosity and began to embrace a kinder and less judgmental attitude. I was starting to be able to let go of needing things to be a certain way, and became less worried about what people might think of how my children behaved. As a new spirit of mutual cooperation arose, we learned to listen to each other and have a very different sense of how a family could be; we were healing each other, one meditation at a time.

Case Study: Alex (aged 4)

My nephew would often ask to practise meditation with me when he came to visit, and we would go up the narrow staircase to my meditation room together, choose a comfortable cushion and a cosy blanket each, and chat a little first so that I could learn what felt relevant and current for him. One day he mentioned that some other children hadn't been kind to him in the playground at school. We talked about how his body felt when that had happened and he showed me his ninja fists, which I understood to mean that he had felt angry. We agreed that anger feels difficult, and after some further discussion, I asked him if he'd like to know the secret to living a happy life. I was planning to reveal the answer with a flourish and divulge my feeling that the secret to happiness is learning to make friends with what feels difficult and bring kindness to ourselves when we're hurting. In an unexpected turn-of-events, however, he shook his head and said that he knew the answer already. As I sat with an undoubted look of slight surprise on my face, he went on to say, "It's connection, isn't it?!" Well, never a truer word was spoken, and I immediately laughed and agreed.

Around two years ago I became a Connected Kids™ Trainer and subsequently also a Mindfulness in Schools Project '.b' and 'Paws b' Teacher. The idea of teaching mindfulness to groups of teenagers absolutely terrified me, but my heart was quite certain that it was my path to do so. Endeavouring to embrace being *way* out of my comfort zone once again, I followed my heart, choosing love over fear. If each of us just remains content to sail around in safe harbour every day, then how would we ever explore new and interesting territory; how would we ever create change? Tough though it is, we have to take a deep breath, ground our attention into *this* body and *this* moment, and push our sails out to catch the wind... not knowing where it will take us but willing to take the ride.

Before I started to teach mindfulness in the high schools I had built up a picture in my head of groups of teenagers as wild, feral creatures who would move in for the proverbial kill at any sign of weakness. I recall delivering the "Taming the Animal Mind" lesson for the first time, where we watched a clip of David

Attenborough interacting with a band of gorillas (the gorillas being a metaphor for our wild animal mind), noticing his attitude as he observed them was one of patient, kind curiosity. He understood the gorillas so well that he was able to be with them in a really skilful and quite inspirational way. We considered that his attitude is the same whether watching a pleasant event or a more difficult one such as a lion capturing and killing an antelope. We talked about how this gives us clues as to how we can be with our wild animal minds in a more skilful way – we can patiently observe, with kindness, getting to know the territory, starting to understand how our minds behave, and bring the same friendly curiosity to the difficult as well as the good. Far from the feral group of teenagers ready to tear me apart, as I looked around the group I was working with each week I saw each young person for who they really were and had such a sense of the common humanity that binds us together. At the root of things, we shared in common the same fears, the same basic wish to be happy, to be healthy, to live with ease. I saw their joy and I saw their suffering – their wrestling with difficulties – just as it is for each of us. I also saw the seeds of present-moment living being sown, and a world of possibilities opening up.

4

Awakening Child

WE ALREADY HAVE everything we need. There is no need for self-improvement.

All these trips that we lay on ourselves – the heavy-duty fearing that we're bad and hoping that we're good, the identities that we so dearly cling to, the rage, the jealousy and the addictions of all kinds – never touch our basic wealth. They are like clouds that temporarily block the sun. But all the time our warmth and brilliance are right here.

This is who we really are.

We are one blink of an eye away from being fully awake.

Pema Chödrön

Our basic wealth – a light that shines so very brightly that we cannot gaze directly upon it. A light that burns with a passion, a potential and a purity. And yet this is not the current day-to-day reality we are faced with. The lives we lead, particularly in the Western world, are technologically overburdened and spiritually impoverished. Our children can tell us the various merits of different operating systems for electronic devices, but are rarely in touch with how different emotions are experienced in the body, or how it feels to bring kindness to a moment of difficulty. They are bombarded almost constantly with information at a rate that mankind even 50 years ago would have struggled to begin to comprehend. Mental illness is at an all-time high; according to the National Institute for Mental Health (NIMH), about 11 per cent of adolescents have a depressive disorder by age 18. Research indicates that one of every four adolescents will have an episode of major depression during high school with the average age of onset being 14 years of age. It is generally accepted that anxiety and depression are amongst the fastest-growing health challenges to our society at present. According to Anxiety UK, anxiety and depression have increased 13% in the UK since 1993, and one in ten children and young people aged 5–16 has a mental health disorder.

The human race is at a tipping point, and *you and I are absolutely pivotal in making the difference between annihilation and awakening.* There is no option, if as a race we wish not only to survive but to flourish, but to do things differently – radically differently. And that's where mindfulness comes in. I believe, or rather *I know* deep down in my heart, that living consciously and moving deeply into the present moment, the only moment that actually exists, is the *only* way forward. Caught up in the pain of what happened to us in the past, the injustices, the needing to be right, the 'eye for an eye and tooth for a tooth' mentality – all of this only leads us further into the mire of suffering. If we are ever to become truly free, and set our children free to fulfil their potential, letting go and moving into the present is the only sane choice we can make. That doesn't mean we have to forget the lessons of the past and accept injustices when they occur with a stoic attitude of 'this person has hurt me badly but never mind', but it does mean that we stay present with our thoughts, emotions and physical sensations exactly as they are, watching them with curiosity and allowing them to arise, be present for as long as they need, and then pass by in their own time. Each time a person lashes out and acts unkindly, they demonstrate unconsciousness – acting out of pain from the past – they are not present. If we meet this unconscious action with presence, truly seeing this person and their pain, we meet hate with love, we bring presence to non-presence, sanity to insanity, healing to disease. *We create the conditions for awakening.*

You may by now be wondering more precisely who and what is this 'Awakening Child', the title of this book? My definition of an awakening child is one who is becoming Aware,

Compassionate and Embodied – learning to live grACEfully. Let's break down these component parts and explore them a little more.

Aware

As human beings, we have the ability not only to think, but also to be aware that we are thinking; this is known as 'metacognition'. So there is an ability not only to do, but to know what we are doing. We may liken this to an image of an observer sitting on a riverbank, watching the river (thoughts, images, emotions, physical sensations) go by. Most of the time we are swimming along in the river, trying to direct what appears to be floating along in it, grasping at thoughts and feelings we like, pushing away and rejecting those we don't like, but just occasionally we are thrust back on to the riverbank and into the present moment – a drop-dead beautiful view stops us in our tracks, we take in the colours of the sky, feel the soft breeze caressing our face, feel our feet against the ground, the sensations of our breath moving in and out of the body, we have a moment of stillness, connectedness. For a fleeting moment, we have remembered. This… just this. This breath. *This* moment. This breath. *This* moment. Can you tune into the parts of your body that are resting against a chair, or bed, or the floor right now, the weight of the body creating sensations of contact and pressure where it's resting against something? Can you tune into the sensations of your breath, allowing them to be just as they are? The in-breath. The out-breath. The space in-between.

4.1 Exercise: Breath Awareness*

Find somewhere comfortable to practise, in a sitting position if possible. Invite the body to adopt a posture that feels strong and supportive, allowing the spine to have its full length (perhaps imagining a silken cord attached to the crown of the head that's being pulled upwards gently), allowing the chin to dip downwards slightly so that the spine at the back of the neck has its full length. Allowing the rest of the body to relax around this strong spine.

Sitting quietly and with your eyes open (if that feels OK).

Setting the intention to be mindful – aware of each moment and without judgement and exploring for a few moments what your personal motivation might be for wishing to develop this faculty of awareness; how might it benefit you, and others in your life?

Now letting go of intention and motivation, and beginning to tune in to the sensations of the breath as if you've never experienced breathing before and bringing a real attitude of curious exploration to this practice, as best you can.

Tuning in to the sensations of the in-breath, allowing the breath to be just as you find it.

Tuning in to the sensations of the out-breath, allowing the breath to be just as you find it.

Noticing any pause between the in-breath and the out-breath, and between the out-breath and in the in-breath.

Perhaps introducing counting now. Counting up to 3 or 4 on the in-breath and the same number of the out-breath, and doing that for a few breaths. So doing two things in this moment – breathing and counting.

If you start to become anxious or tense with the counting, then let the counting go and just focus on the sensations of the breath entering and leaving the body. Maybe you're aware of cool air rushing past the insides of the nostrils as you breathe in, maybe you can feel warm air rushing past the insides of the nostrils as you breathe out, or maybe the lips. Perhaps there are sensations of stretching in the belly with the in-breath, perhaps movement in the shoulders, the chest, the back.

Letting go of any counting now. Watching the tide of the breath. The tide rolls in... the tide turns... the tide rolls out... the tide turns. Riding the waves of the breath for a few moments.

Taking a moment now to tune into how the mind feels right now – does it feel busy, or spacious, or somewhere in-between? No wrong answer, just noticing.

Tip: to deliver the above meditation to a child, adjust the language a little (as appropriate for their age and stage of development), and use engaging metaphor. For example:

Invite your body to find a comfortable sitting position that feels tall and strong like a mountain. Allowing your spine – that's the column of bones in the middle of your back – to have its full length and asking the rest of your body to relax around this strong spine.

Sitting quietly and perhaps allowing your eyes to close, if that feels OK. If you'd prefer to keep your eyes open, then softening your gaze by looking out through the sides of your eyes.

Decide to pay attention to the present moment with a kind and curious attitude, like an explorer.

Beginning to tune in to how it feels to breathe now, as if you've never experienced breathing before. Perhaps imagine that you're like a radio, tuning into sensations that pop up in the body for your attention. Tuning in to any sensations of movement in the chest as you breathe in and out, or in the shoulders, or maybe in the tummy. Are there any sensations of stretching in the tummy as you breathe in? Answering any questions in your head and then we can perhaps talk about them afterwards if you'd like to.

Perhaps moving your hands in time with your breath now, stretching out the palms of your hands as you breathe in and closing your hands as you breathe out by bringing the fingers of the hand towards the thumb.

Opening the hands on the in-breath, and closing them on the out-breath.

So doing two things in this moment – breathing and moving your hands in time with your breathing, in whatever way feels right for you. <You may wish to ask the child to do this for 5 complete breaths, or longer if they seem really settled.>

Letting go of any movement of the hands now, and just feeling the movement of the breath. Perhaps you can feel the cooler air tickling the insides of your nostrils as you breathe in? Perhaps you're aware of the warmer air passing through your nostrils as you breathe out, and maybe you can feel this warm air touching the area above your top lip.

Taking a moment now to tune into how your mind feels right now – does it feel busy like a loud party, quiet like a library, or somewhere in-between? No wrong answer, just noticing.

Case Study: Sarah (aged 14)

As is the alarming outlet for all too many teenagers these days, stresses and anxieties in Sarah's life had become so overwhelming that she had been self-harming as a way of releasing tension. We met for a weekly 40-minute session for nine weeks as she became more familiar with the workings of her mind and learned to ground her attention into the body and drop anchor there, watching the breath and other sensations. After several weeks of working together, when I enquired how her home practice had been over the previous week, she responded with such a happy facial expression and a real sense of wonder in her voice, telling me that her breath was always her enemy until she learned mindfulness, but that now it was her friend. She previously would notice when she felt panicky that her heart was racing and that her breathing was shallow and ragged – it wasn't how she wanted it to be but she couldn't control it, and so the feeling of overwhelm and lack of control grew even stronger. Now her breath was her early-warning-system, letting her know when she was starting to get anxious, and then she knew to deepen her breathing for a few breaths and then just gently focus on riding the waves of the breath. In addition, she reported that catching the anxiety earlier as it arose, often during the school day, gave her the space to choose how best to respond to the situation and be kind to herself rather than her old behaviour of reacting without thinking (which usually involved just running out of the room and having, in her words, a 'meltdown').

Compassionate

Clive Holmes of the Mindfulness Association gives us a wonderful insight into the nature of compassion when he explains, "When the sunshine of loving kindness meets the tears of suffering, then the rainbow of compassion is born." We can teach children what it means to be kind, and also what it means to be compassionate, through our way of being; as we move kindly and compassionately through the world, so a child can learn what it looks like to do so.

My research into teaching mindfulness to children, as part of my training for the Postgraduate Diploma in Mindfulness Studies and my PhD thesis, has really enforced my motivation to promote compassion as being at the heart of any mindfulness training for children. If we only promote development of single-faceted mindfulness (just focusing on calmer minds and an ability to sustain attention) then I strongly argue that an opportunity is missed and that we do the child a disservice. Mindfulness creates a greater awareness of the content of the mind, and so we must nurture self-compassion in order to have the inner resources to face the difficulties that are revealed, those emotions we'd rather not feel, those thoughts we'd rather not have. Paul Gilbert, author of *Mindful Compassion* and *The Compassionate Mind*, supports this view of the importance of self-compassion within education, telling us, "There is no question whatsoever now that compassion can be and should be at the heart of all that we do – at the heart of our education and how we treat and teach our children." It may actually be that self-compassion is more strongly predictive of psychological health than single-faceted mindfulness (mindfulness that relates only to calm awareness).

Dr Kristen Neff, a pioneer of research into self-compassion over the past 15 years or so and Associate Professor at the University of Texas at Austin, proposes that self-compassion has three main elements – kindness, common humanity and mindfulness. Her research very much backs the view that self-compassion is strongly linked to psychological well-being; those with higher levels of self-compassion are likely to be more optimistic, happier, less anxious, have a greater sense of common humanity, and are also less likely to be depressed and become caught up in rumination. Her research also points to self-compassion as being highly relevant to adolescents given the nature of the process of this stage of development where identity formation is key: bodies are changing, there is a tendency to be deeply concerned with what others think of them, there may be a strong desire to 'fit in', relationships may be in flux, academic pressures can feel overwhelming.

When we consider how much change any child goes through from birth to adolescence, it really seems a no-brainer to make self-compassion the absolute foundation of what we teach our children in all stages of the education system. And how beneficial too for teacher training to be built upon a foundation of self-compassion. The word 'self-esteem' is often used in relation to the well-being of our children, but Neff's research highlights how focusing on increasing self-esteem can be problematic; she suggests that self-compassion may have similar mental health benefits to self-esteem but without the potential pitfalls. She argues that: "Self-compassion provides greater emotional resilience and stability than self-esteem, but involves less self-evaluation, ego-defensiveness, and self-enhancement than self-esteem." She goes on to say that, "Whereas self-esteem entails evaluating oneself positively and often involves the need to be special and above average, self-compassion does not entail self-evaluation or comparisons with others. Rather, it is a kind, connected, and clear-sighted way of relating to ourselves even in instances of failure, perceived inadequacy, and imperfection."

I hope that by now I've presented a compelling case for recognising the value of teaching children self-compassion, i.e. to direct kindness towards their difficulties. In order to do this, we have some work to do, because we have to be able to do this for ourselves before we can teach it to others!

[Kids] don't remember what you try to teach them. They remember what you are.
Jim Henson, *It's Not Easy Being Green: And Other Things to Consider*

We are taught to be kind to others, because that's what nice people do. I don't recall being taught to be kind to myself, but I do remember feeling guilty as a child when adults chastised me for not being kind or compassionate when they felt I ought to be (for example, Jenny stole my ball but I was told I should be kind and understanding because her mother had recently left the family; I felt angry, hurt and most of all confused, because I was indirectly being shown that these feelings were clearly wrong because I should be offering compassion to Jenny). Unfortunately, we can only offer genuine kindness and compassion to others to the extent that we can offer *ourselves* kindness and compassion, so the model of teaching children to focus on being kind to others is rather flawed – we may have children who behave in a way that outwardly appears kind because it is what is expected of them, it's what 'nice' people do, or because they hope that it will ingratiate them with the person they're offering kindness to, rather than because loving-kindness naturally flows to self and others.

Here is an exercise that works with the intention of growing self-compassion and may help you to explore the felt sense of loving-kindness in the body. I'll be inviting you to bring to mind in the exercise someone with whom you have a relatively uncomplicated relationship and someone who has unconditional positive regard for you – someone who has your best interests at heart. It could be a dear friend, a favourite aunt, or even a pet! In fact, it doesn't even need to be a real live person; you may prefer to bring to mind a compassionate being from whichever faith you follow. I'll call them "your compassionate friend".

4.2 Exercise: Self-Compassionate Intention*

Find somewhere comfortable to practise where you're unlikely to be disturbed.

As you bring your attention to the breath, intend to connect to a soothing breathing rhythm; perhaps watching the tide of the breath as it rolls in and rolls out, just as we might watch waves rolling in and out on the seashore. Observing the flow of the breath, and inviting the body to soften and flow, saying the words over and over again in the mind's eye, "Soften and flow, soften and flow, soften and flow."

Allowing our experience to be just as it is, and intending to relate to whatever our experience is with a soothing warmth and a genuine kindness. Just working with intention (so not needing our inner experience to be different from how it is) and being aware that whilst warmth and kindness may not be part of our experience right now, we would like them to be. It is enough to simply have the intention to grow the seed of compassion within us – setting the direction of our travel – and then let the journey unfold.

Aware of the weight of the body as it rests here, noticing the points of contact between the body and whatever it's resting on.

And perhaps imagining now that you're in a beautiful garden, somewhere that feels really quite special, and either visualising this place or simply having a felt sense of being there. Observing any sensations arising in the body as you fill in some of the details of this place in your mind's eye, noticing any sounds, sights, textures and aromas in this garden, and perhaps having a sense that this is a truly benevolent place – a place that genuinely wishes the best for you.

In the centre of the garden, in a beautiful rockery with a little fountain in the middle, you notice an array of flowers of every colour and see a space in their midst where the soil looks newly readied for planting. As you take your attention to your hands, you realise that a small seed rests in the centre of one of your palms, and you recognise it as the seed of self-compassion. This seed represents your wish to cultivate an ability to direct kindness to yourself in times of difficulty. How would it feel to plant that seed in the space that awaits it?

If it would feel OK, then imagine kneeling down on the ground now and carefully pushing the seed gently into the soil, an inch or two down, and then covering the seed over with a little soil, having a sense that the seed of self-compassion has now been planted with care and love.

As you look up from where you are kneeling, you may have a sense that your compassionate friend has joined you and was actually there all along as you planted your seed. As you look up at their face, you see such a softness, such a warmth, such a genuine expression of loving-kindness gazing back at you. How does it feel in the body to be in the presence of your compassionate friend? Any sensations that you're now aware of? Your compassionate friend feels such joy to have watched you plant the seed of your intention to be kinder to yourself and wants you to know that this garden will look after your seed but you must visit and tend the seed regularly to help it to flourish and grow strong roots.

Finish by taking a moment to reflect on how sorely this world needs more compassion. Remembering that we can only direct compassion towards others to the extent that we can do this for ourselves, and so the benefits of growing self-compassion will ripple outwards and touch all those we connect with, in ever-widening circles.

Tip: you can guide a teen in the above meditation pretty much as it is, but I would avoid leading a group of teens in this practice unless they've been practising mindfulness for a little while. As a variation on the theme, younger children may enjoy a 'Kind Wishes' mindful activity that involves tracing and cutting out paper doves which are symbols of peace. You can suggest that the child writes on each dove the name of a person or group of people (or animal) they'd like to send kind wishes to. Encourage the child to include themselves and write their own name on one of the doves. You can then string the doves together and pin them on a wall, or laminate them before stringing them together and you can hang them outside on a tree or a bush in your garden. Alternatively, you could create a 'tree of peace' – drawing a tree on a large piece of paper and then decorating the tree with the doves.

Embodied

Before I learned mindfulness, I felt very much like a lollipop-head – my head was the giant lollipop and my body was the stick. There was quite a disconnect between my head and the rest of me, and I rarely paused to think about my body unless it was letting me down by getting sick, sore, or tired. Mindfulness is very much about inviting the energy of the mind to move away from *just* residing in the head and instead residing in the *whole* of the body and thus training ourselves to move from thinking mode into sensing mode. Not because there's anything wrong with thinking – it's a very useful faculty – but because we're almost always in *thinking* mode and have forgotten how to be in *sensing* mode. This cuts us off from a massive part of ourselves and a massive source of strength and wisdom. In *sensing* mode, we are like Weebles – we might wobble with life's knocks but we don't fall down. There is a stability in allowing the mind to fully inhabit the body. In *thinking* mode, we are like lollipops; we don't have great balance and if you did manage to get a lollipop to balance on its stick then the slightest breeze or knock would make it fall! We in the Western world are very much led by our rational, logical, *thinking* mode of mind, but actually it is much more powerful to allow the *sensing* mode of mind to guide how we move through life with the *thinking* mode following the lead of the *sensing* mode.

4.3 Exercise: Sensing Mode*

Find somewhere comfortable to practise where you're unlikely to be disturbed.

Beginning by setting the intention to pay close attention to what arises in the mind in relation to the senses of touch, sound, taste, smell and sight and simply let go of any need to do anything – not even trying to meditate; simply allowing the body and the mind to just be.

Then following the steps of the Breath Awareness exercise from earlier: tuning into the sensations of the breath as they're being experienced in the body in this moment and perhaps introducing counting if you find that helpful – breathe in to a count of 3 or 4, and breathing out to the same number.

After a short while, letting go of any counting and starting to invite the mind to occupy the whole body. Becoming aware of the weight of the body creating sensations of contact and pressure between the body and whatever it's resting against and really observing with a sense of curiosity what that feels like in this moment. Really tuning into the ever-changing landscape of sensation with a beginner's mind, as if you've only just noticed that you have a body! What are the patterns of sensation that make up what we call 'contact' and 'pressure'?

If you take your attention into your feet, in this moment, what sensations are available to be noticed? Don't worry if you can't feel anything in particular – just being curious. What about your hands? Noticing any sensations created by contact between the hands and whatever they're resting against. How does that feel?

Taking your attention to the changes in the body now as the breath enters... and leaves. What are the changing patterns of sensation in the body in relation to the breath entering and leaving? Are there any sensations to be noticed in the nostrils? In the chest? In the back? In the belly? Just observing with curiosity and warmth.

Having a sense of really inhabiting the whole of this body – this body that does so much for us every moment of every day, generally with little thanks, and always doing its best to come back into balance. Feeling into it from the inside rather than thinking about it. As this body rests here, trusting in the support of the ground beneath it, perhaps the mind can start to really trust this body as a place to come home to and rest in. Resting here, aware of the space around and maybe also having a sense of space within the body – space within which the mind can rest – and tuning into remaining senses now.

Noticing any taste in the mouth. Is there any aroma to become aware of? Are there any sound waves reaching the ears in this moment? Tuning into the silence if not.

Without moving the head, noticing any visual information that is currently being received by the eyes.

Finishing by setting the intention to bring this quality of awareness into the remainder of your day.

Another practice that can really bring us into Weeble mode is the Body Scan. Undoubtedly one of the most famous mindfulness practices, practising it regularly will really enhance your ability to tune into what is real and true for you in any moment, as reflected in the body. It's quite a lengthy practice, taking up to 45 minutes or so, and one that many people (including me) enjoy sometimes as a precursor to sleep as it's so wonderfully relaxing. I've included an example of a body scan that's suitable for younger children in Chapter 16 (16.4 Where's my Body?) and a version for teens (17.3 Bodykind) in Chapter 17.

4.4 Exercise: Body Scan*

Find somewhere comfortable to practise where you're unlikely to be disturbed, and lie down if you can, choosing a posture that is kind to the body and as comfortable as possible. You may wish to lie flat on your back, perhaps with knees bent to take some pressure off the lower back and with your toes turned a little inwards to help the knees to support each other. If the legs are flat against the floor, then allow the feet to flop away from each other so that the legs are completely relaxed. If you can, allow your arms to rest a little way away from the rest of your body.

Beginning by setting an intention with this practice to allow the body to relax as fully as possible. And then once we've fired the arrow of our intention, we just let go of needing our experience to be a certain way. Allowing, as best we can, our experience to unfold moment-by-moment, letting go of judgement, letting go of critical thoughts. Making best endeavours to allow the body to be just as we find it.

Becoming aware of the weight of this body as it rests here, the force of gravity creating sensations of contact and pressure, and noticing what those sensations actually feel like in this moment. Becoming aware of the whole of the body from the soles of the feet, right up to the crown of the head. Aware of the whole of the body from the back of the body right through to the front. Aware of the whole of the body from one side, right across to the other side. Tuning in to the sensations of the breath as we lie here. Noticing what the in-breath feels like. Perhaps this is the first time you've paid attention to your breath today. Noticing what the sensations of the out-breath feel like, and noticing any tendency of the body to relax a little bit on the out-breath. With each out-breath, maybe inviting the body to let go even more – to really let go into the support of the ground beneath. Inviting the body to sink a little bit deeper into whatever you're lying on, and perhaps taking a moment to congratulate yourself for having carved out this time to simply be with this body – to allow this body to rest, and to allow this body to be just as you find it.

In this practice we're going to be gently, and with curiosity, taking our attention around the body, visiting various different body parts. If there's any body part that you just don't feel like paying attention to right now, then that's absolutely fine – you can either skip to the next body part or simply rest your attention on the sensations of the breathing until we've moved on. Just trusting yourself to know what's right for you and being aware that there's absolutely no wrong way to do this practice.

Set the intention to remain alert, kind, and intensely curious about your experience as it unfolds, moment-to-moment. Each time you notice that the mind has wandered off into the past, the future, or into daydreaming, patiently, kindly and firmly bring it back to whichever body part we're focusing on.

Taking your attention now into the toes of the left foot, and if you're not sure which foot is your left then just choose a foot. Taking all of your attention as best you can into the toes of the left foot and noticing what sensations are here, if any, to be noticed. Perhaps there are sensations of tingling, buzzing, or glowing. Maybe sensations of warmth, or coolness. Maybe sensations of contact where the toes are touching each other. If you're not aware of any sensations then just registering a blank, at any point. Perhaps imagining breathing in to these toes now – all of the toes of the left foot – and that might feel like a rather strange thing to do, but just approaching this with curiosity and patience, as best you can. So, as you breathe in, imagine that the air travels into the lungs and down through the body and out to the toes of the left foot. Then as you breathe out, the breath travels back up the leg, up to the chest, and out through the nostrils or the mouth. Experimenting with breathing that way for a few breaths.

Each time we move our attention to another body part, you may want to explore directing the breathing into that body part. For now, on the next out-breath, allowing the toes of the left foot to just dissolve gently in the mind's eye.

Inviting the attention now into the sides of the left foot, the sole of the left foot, the top of the left foot. Tuning in to all of the bones in that left foot, the muscles, the blood vessels, tendons and ligaments, and skin surrounding. Just noting any physical sensations that are there to be noticed in this moment. And on the next out-breath, letting go of the awareness of that left foot.

Placing your attention now into the left ankle and seeing if there's anything here to be noticed. How does your left ankle feel right now?

And then on the next out-breath letting go of that ankle. Inviting the attention now into the left lower leg, from just above the left ankle to just below the left knee. Tuning into those strong bones of the lower leg, the muscles, tendons, ligaments, blood vessels, and skin surrounding. Tuning in to each and every cell in that area of the body, as best we can, and seeing if there's any sense of aliveness here – anything that you can detect. And reminding yourself that there's no wrong way to feel; whatever your experience is, is the right experience.

On the next out-breath, allowing the left lower leg to simply dissolve in the mind's eye.

Bringing our attention now into the left knee, noticing what physical sensations, if any, are here to be noticed. If at any point you experience intense sensations during the practice, then perhaps directing the breath to that area and inviting the body to soften around that intensity – not as a way of making anything go away, but as a way of relating more skilfully to what's here anyway. So tending to any area of intensity that really calls strongly for your attention, and then returning your attention to whichever body part we were resting on – wherever we were placing our attention. For just now, placing the attention in that left knee, tuning in to whatever sensations are here in this moment.

Then on the next out-breath letting go of the left knee.

Inviting your attention to move into the left thigh now, from just above that left knee up to the hip bone on the outside of the thigh and up to the groin on the inside of the thigh. Maybe aware of sensations of contact and pressure where the thigh is resting against anything. Maybe aware of sensations of clothing or a blanket resting against the thigh.

Then on the next out-breath, letting go of the left thigh and moving your attention now out to the right foot, including in your field of awareness the toes of the right foot, the sole, the sides of the foot, the top of the foot, and inside of that foot (including all of those little bones and joints). Perhaps including the right ankle as well. Tuning into the right foot with a beginner's mind – a mind that's willing to not know, to not have all the answers, to not make assumptions.

On the next out-breath, letting go of that right foot and right ankle, and moving your attention into the right lower leg now from just above the ankle to just below the knee. What physical sensations are here to be noticed right now? And on the next out-breath, letting go of that right lower leg.

Inviting your attention to rest now in the right knee. Tuning in to the right knee from the inside. And on the next out-breath, letting go of the right knee.

Moving the attention into the right thigh now, from just above the right knee up to the hip bone on the outside and up to the groin on *the inside. What physical sensations are here to be noticed, right now? And on the next out-breath, letting go of the right thigh.*

Moving your awareness now to the groin, the buttocks, the pelvis. What sensations are here to be noticed, in this moment? Any sensations of contact, where the buttocks meet whatever you're lying on? If so, what does that contact actually feel like, right now? And including in your awareness the organs of this area – the reproductive organs and large intestine, all cradled in that pelvic area. And on the next out-breath allowing this area of the body to gently dissolve in the mind's eye.

Inviting your attention into the lower back now, to the very base of the spine. From that part of the spine that joins the pelvis, moving up vertebra by vertebra, up the spinal column, right up to the base of the neck. Expanding your field of awareness to include the whole of the back now, so radiating your attention out from that central spine. How does the back feel right now? Perhaps there are areas of the back that are in contact with something that you're lying on? Perhaps also areas of the back that aren't in contact with anything, or maybe there are sensations of clothing resting against those parts. Maybe there are areas of discomfort in the back. Remembering that we can always choose to adjust our position, if that would feel kind to the body, but bringing mindful awareness – as best we can – to any change in position, so really seeing if we can open ourselves to the intense sensation and exploring exactly how it feels. Seeing if we can do that without any judgement. And then with full awareness, making an adjustment to the position of the body that feels helpful. And on the next out-breath, allowing the back to dissolve in the mind's eye.

Bringing your attention now into the stomach area. Perhaps aware of small stretching sensations on the in-breath in the area of the stomach. Tuning in to the internal organs of that area as well as the skin surrounding. And on the next out-breath, letting go of this region of the body.

Bringing the attention now into the chest area, perhaps having a felt sense of the diaphragm flattening to allow the air to enter the lungs; the lungs filling, and then the diaphragm returning to its dome-shape, the breath forced out of the lungs. Those movements in the chest area – perhaps a rise and a fall – the ribs moving a little bit further away from each other on the in-breath; coming closer together on the out-breath. Aware of the organs in this area – tuning into the heart and the lungs. And on the next out-breath, letting go of the chest area and allowing it to simply dissolve in the mind's eye.

Bringing your attention into the shoulders now. Including in your field of awareness the fronts of the shoulders, the backs of the shoulders, tuning in to the shoulder joints and the shoulder blades, the tops of the arms. Either paying attention to one arm at a time or both arms together – whichever you find most helpful. Including the elbows and the lower arms, the wrists, the palms of the hands, the backs of the hands, the thumbs and the fingers. Tuning in to all of those bones and muscles, tendons and ligaments, joints and blood vessels, tissue surrounding the muscles, the skin encasing all of that. Tuning into how your shoulders and arms, wrists and hands feel, right now. On the next out-breath, letting go of the shoulders and the arms.

Bringing the attention into the neck and throat now, tuning in to how they feel, and then expanding the awareness to include the jaw, the tongue, the lips, the roof of the mouth, the rest of the inside of the mouth and the teeth. Including the nose, the cheeks, the eyes, the eyelids, the eyebrows, the forehead, the whole of the top of the head, the sides of the head (including the ears), the back of the head. Perhaps aware of sensations of contact and pressure if the head is resting against a pillow or cushion or something else, and tuning in to the whole of the skull, the sinuses, the brain, the spinal column as it passes through the back of the neck. Holding the neck, the throat and the whole of the head, including the face, in our awareness, and noticing what sensations are here to be noticed. Perhaps imagining directing the breath into the head, breathing into the head and breathing out from the head. Noticing how that feels. And on the next out-breath letting go of awareness of the head, neck and throat, and inviting our field of awareness to encompass the whole of the body now.

Becoming aware of the whole of the body from the top of the head right down to the soles of the feet. Becoming aware of the whole of the body from the front right through to the back. Becoming aware of the whole of the body from one side right across to the other side.

Having a sense of the whole of this body lying here, breathing, and spending some time being in touch with the qualities of the in-breath (those of nourishing, renewing, replenishing, invigorating) and the qualities of the out-breath (purifying, detoxifying, letting go of what we no longer need).

Thanking yourself for having taken the time to be in stillness with the body and the mind – a nurturing time, a healing time – and finishing by perhaps having a sense of wholeness, of completeness, of innate 'OKness'.

So through all of these practices, and indeed the remainder of the book, we are learning to guide our child on this journey of awakening (and thus awaken ourselves). We are finding our way back home to nature – have you noticed that when we are in nature our heads often seem to feel 'clearer' and we often gain a new perspective on a situation? Each thought that we have is an electrical impulse, a movement of energy, and this energy spends most of its time burbling around in the head, unable to free itself as we chew on the same thoughts, over and over, in the misguided view that this will lead to a new perspective. Nature evokes a sense of wonder, and encourages us to use all of our senses, dropping into sensing mode – the place from which a new perspective will arrive. Amidst the beauty of nature, it is almost impossible to stay in a contracted state, holding on to the hard shell of *me* and the need to control what happens to me. Nature announces over and over again the impermanence of things, teaching us that all things change, that control is an illusion, and that all life is cyclical in nature. We are finding our way back home to the experience of the body in this moment, learning to be unafraid to experience difficult emotions and to approach them with curiosity and a sense of allowing. We are reminding ourselves that our emotions are not the direct result of someone else's actions, but because of our thoughts about that action. We are learning how it feels to be fully present for each other. And finally, we are coming home to a sense of connectedness and beginning to see the illusion of perceiving ourselves as separate little islands moving through life.

5

Understanding Stress

Peace is the result of retraining your mind to process life as it is, rather than as you think it should be.
Dr Wayne Dyer

In the next chapter we'll delve more deeply into what mindfulness, meditation and visualisation are and how they relate to each other, but first of all it's perhaps worthwhile exploring what stress actually is and how the body deals with it – we can then better understand why mindfulness, meditation and visualisation can make such an impact on our experience of stress. You're perhaps quite familiar, as most of us are (and especially if you're a parent), with how stress feels in the body? Maybe for you it's a tension that's held in the shoulders or the jaw? Or maybe it's sensations of tightness in the tummy, along with shallower breathing and a woolly or foggy head. It's often accompanied by feelings of an inability to cope, of being *overwhelmed*. This is what it feels like when the stress response has not run its course in the way that it was designed to do. Stress is a normal physiological response to physical danger. It's an extremely useful response that one day may save your life as you leap out of the way of an oncoming car, for example. Life can feel like slow motion in those moments, with intense clarity. Those are not moments when it would be useful to have the higher functioning part of the brain involved – that part of the brain that processes and analyses information, that can do algebra and work out the relative merits of different routes from A to B. Those are moments when physical strength and effectively instantaneous response are required so that we can fight what threatens us or run away from it. This kind of stress is acute stress, and it's the kind that has helped us to survive.

These days, the stressful situations that we encounter are rarely of the physical danger kind where a sabre-toothed tiger is lurking around the corner – they are far more likely to be centred around our situation at work (maybe a deadline coming up, or not getting on with a colleague) or at home (e.g. worries about finances, relationship difficulties, bickering children). Often the threats we perceive are self-made – we may see a friend across the road and wave, only to find our gesture being unacknowledged. Depending on our mood and what else is going on in our life, we may choose to think that perhaps our friend didn't see us, or alternatively that this friend was deliberately being rude – this latter thought may lead down a long road of analysing *why*; we might even start to get angry with our friend, or maybe really sad that we feel we've now lost our friend. Whether a sudden physical danger is presenting, or a worry about work or home life, the response in the body is still almost exactly the same, but the nature of the trigger is very different and it's easy to see why stress in modern times becomes chronic because the triggers (unlike sudden physical dangers) don't go away in a short space of time.

Evolution really hasn't helped us with regard to dealing with stressors. Think of a herd of antelope grazing peacefully on the savannah when a hunting lion makes a sudden dash to capture one of them; the herd scatters, the sudden release of adrenaline propelling the antelope into lightning-fast reaction, but the lion manages to take one of the herd down and it's lights out for the poor antelope. *Moments later the herd is grazing again.* For us, with a higher-functioning 'new brain' or neocortex essentially built around the 'old brain' we wouldn't be able to relax any time soon and start eating. We'd quite understandably be worrying about where the lion might pop up next... "It was so fast! I don't feel safe. I'm worried that my family isn't safe. What if it had been my child who was taken?" We might find the mind moving into persistent cycles of worry about lions until every swaying blade of grass becomes a potential threat.

I'm a bit of a geek (you may have already come to this conclusion, considering my earlier career as a software engineer) and really fascinated by the workings of the human body. From age four until age seventeen I was very set on becoming a doctor so that I could rid the world of cancer (a lofty aim, I know, but I'm not prone to dreaming small), however, upon entering medical school I quickly realised that the idea of focusing on treating symptoms made little sense to me and my medical studies only lasted for one year. My keen interest in the miracle of the body has remained though, and so I will go into the process of the stress response in more detail in the remainder of this chapter. I hope that you'll stay with me as I delve a little deeper into what's actually going on in the body, because understanding a little of the science behind our human experience can also help to motivate us in our practice – we start to link elements of our practice to what is happening in the brain and the rest of the body and can start to see *why* some of the practices outlined in this book can make a difference. It is also worth mentioning that children really love learning 'wow words' like amygdala, hippocampus and hypothalamus, and it can give them a really useful perspective on what's actually happening when we experience stressful situations and how the body processes emotions.

You may remember from biology lessons at school that the sympathetic nervous system (SNS) functions like the accelerator in a car. It is the 'fight-or-flight' wing of the autonomic nervous system, providing the body with a sudden burst of energy so that it can react to perceived dangers. The parasympathetic nervous system acts like the brakes on the car and is the 'rest and digest' wing of the autonomic nervous system. It causes the body to return to equilibrium once the perceived threat has passed.

If we consider the normal stress response triggered by, say, a car approaching alarmingly fast as we're crossing the road, we can see that the event triggers a cascading reaction, and following the action (which is 'fight', 'flight', or if the mind feels that survival is unlikely then there's also 'freeze') the parasympathetic nervous system kicks in and the body returns to 'normal'. We can also see that there's actually an awful lot going on and it's happening remarkably quickly – much more quickly than conscious thought. When something stressful occurs, *real or imagined*, the process is as follows:

1. There's a deepening attention to stimulus – the nerve circuitry becomes physically more sensitive and active.
2. The amygdala (emotional processing) and hippocampus (associated with memory access) flag the stimulus as good, bad or neutral.
3. The amygdala, upon flagging the stimulus as bad, sends a distress signal to the hypothalamus.
4. The hypothalamus acts rather like a command centre and activates the sympathetic nervous system (SNS) by sending signals through the autonomic nerves to the adrenal glands. The adrenal glands respond by pumping adrenaline into the bloodstream.
5. As adrenaline circulates through the body, there are numerous physiological changes. The heart rate increases, encouraging blood flow to the heart, muscles and other vital organs. Blood pressure goes up and the breathing becomes more rapid to cope with the increased demand for oxygen. Small airways in the lungs dilate so that as much oxygen as possible can transfer to the blood via the lungs with each breath; the brain receives extra oxygen and becomes more alert. Senses become sharper.
6. The circulating adrenaline triggers the body to release glucose and fats from temporary storage sites in the body into the bloodstream so that the body receives a boost in

energy that is needed for sudden and violent muscular action: fighting or running away. All of these steps happen very rapidly – so fast indeed that the amygdala and hypothalamus start the reaction even before the brain has fully interpreted the image of what is happening!

7. As the initial surge of adrenaline subsides, the hypothalamus triggers the next component of the stress response system. If the situation is still perceived by the brain to be threatening, then a sequence of chemical messengers is released that causes the adrenal glands to start releasing cortisol and the accelerator of the car stays pressed down – the body remains on high alert.

8. When the threat passes, cortisol levels fall and the parasympathetic nervous system – the brakes of the car – then begins to bring the body back to equilibrium by dampening the stress response.

For many of us, the accelerator of the car stays pressed down much of the time. Both external and internally-created pressures keep us in a chronic state of low-level stress that spikes to higher levels intermittently. We know that prolonged stress is bad for us – it causes the body and mind innumerable problems including high blood pressure, inflammation, weakened immune system, infertility, sleep problems, increased risk of heart disease, increased likelihood of depression and anxiety, and contributes perhaps towards obesity (through both comfort eating and also elevated cortisol levels causing increased appetite). But although we're aware of how it's harming us, most of us are fairly clueless about how to reduce our stress and live the life we are destined to live; many turn to alcohol as a form of 'relaxation' and a way of letting go of the stresses of the day, and many rely on 'future-living' as a crutch to limp through life with, living for the weekends (with the inevitable low mood on a Sunday evening) and finding the next holiday to look forward to, feeling rather miserable immediately after a holiday until the next one is booked. It's worth reminding ourselves at this point that some stress is unavoidable and often quite useful in focusing and empowering us to perform well, so we're not looking for ways to rid ourselves of stress completely, but instead we are looking to avoid adding unnecessarily to our experience of stress with our thoughts and also at ways of activating the parasympathetic nervous system and helping the amygdala to learn to chill out.

Perhaps the most important thing, when realising you've been living with chronic stress and wishing to rebalance, is not to get stressed out about feeling stressed – I'm sure you can see why! This is why the attitude of acceptance, discussed in Chapter 9, is so fundamental to learning a new way of being; when we resist what *is* we create further stress and feed the negative energy state with more energy. Carl Jung, the eminent Swiss psychiatrist and psychotherapist who founded analytical psychology, wisely pointed out, "What you resist not only persists, but will grow in size." At its most basic level, chronic stress is where we find ourselves in place or situation A but wish to be in place or situation B. The tension between A and B is stress. If we can find ourselves at A, with a preference to be at B but *allowing life to be just as it is* and accepting that A is where we are, warts 'n' all, then we will have let go of suffering. It's really worth clarifying at this point that what I'm talking about here are *internal* states of resistance; there is no suggestion that it's OK if someone is being violent towards us, for example, and it doesn't mean that we can't take steps to change our situation, but we do so from a place of complete non-resistance to the thoughts and emotions that are here in this moment and from a place of compassion. Tara Brach calls this "Radical Acceptance" in her book of the same name. We are then in complete *alignment with life*.

Case Study: Billy (aged 14)

I was working for some time with a delightful young man with a wicked sense of humour who'd been suffering with depression and anxiety for many years. He had been seeing a psychologist for approximately one year, and had apparently been learning that many of his feelings were undesirable and 'wrong' and they had been looking at ways that he might be able to change his feelings. In our first session together we talked of all emotions being OK to experience; we can allow them all. Some of them might feel uncomfortable, some of them might feel much more pleasant, and there are unhelpful ways to deal with them (for example, lashing out or trashing his room) and helpful ways of being in relationship with them (to notice they're there, and bring kind and curious attention to them). His body language visibly relaxed quite dramatically during this conversation – his body mirroring the acceptance he was hearing and feeling – and after a 10-minute breath awareness practice he looked as if a huge weight had been lifted from his shoulders. His mother commented that it was the happiest she had seen him in a great many months.

Children and Stress

Children's lives are absolutely full of stress! Parents are often surprised to hear this, wondering how a child's stress over not having been picked as 'Star of the Week' for good behaviour could possibly compare to the stress of worrying about paying household bills. Yet children are faced with numerous pressures that are every bit as challenging, if not more so, than those that adults face. At least we, as adults, always have the power to make choices for ourselves – children often feel powerless in this respect. Children are:

- striving to fit in, and seeking to understand who they are,
- told what to do and how to behave,
- physically changing and developing, often at a different rate to their peers,
- learning how to conduct relationships, often struggling

with siblings, and learning how to balance fulfilling their own needs with an awareness of the needs of others,

- increasingly detached from reality because of the prevalence of computer games and virtual reality (SMS, e-mail, social media),
- aware of world events through the news and social media, and often unaware of the negative bias shown by most reporting agencies – as a society we are much more captivated by the bad stories than by the good ones,
- affected by marketing and advertising – striving to attain that 'perfect' image of the air-brushed celebrities on the front of their favourite magazine and perhaps less able to discern than adults the ways in which such images can mislead,
- embedded in many ways in the lives of their parents and, as such, parental behaviour has a profound influence on the child. Children pick up on the worries of their parents or carers (and even to some extent their teachers – particularly in primary schools where each child often works almost entirely under the guidance of one teacher for the whole school year) and can feel the tension in the household when there are arguments, worries over finances or family fallouts, or worries over current world events, even if they're not able to understand the details. The financial pressures and stresses on parents at present could be argued to be greater than at any time since perhaps World War II.

So in essence, it is all too easy for children to feel disempowered, confused, ungrounded and insecure. You may be starting to have a sense that mindfulness could be the most wonderful medicine for all of this, but if indeed children are so affected by the stress and the behaviour of their parents and those around them, then we can also start to see how the benefits of transforming *ourselves* through mindfulness can play out.

In the 1990s some New Zealand scientists, along with a biologist named Michael Meaney, discovered a strong link between the behaviour of mother rats and their young. Some young rats displayed very anxious, fearful behaviour and others would display very relaxed, approach-based behaviour. The mothers were switched so that anxious young rats were then parented by relaxed mothers and vice versa. The anxious young rats, when parented by relaxed mothers, grew up to be relaxed and curious rats, whereas the relaxed young rats when parented by neurotic mothers grew up to be anxious and fearful. This is nurture over nature. Meaney went on to show that this wasn't simply learned behaviour and that hormone receptors had actually been switched on or off in response to the experience of the rats.

It is powerful to realise that even if we are genetically predisposed to an anxiety, depression or some other ailment, our experiences in life are what determine whether or not these genes are activated. It is also humbling to realise how much of our own behaviour affects children whose care we are responsible for, and underlines how very important it is that we find ways to bring ourselves more into balance.

Jon Kabat-Zinn in his wonderful book, *Full Catastrophe Living*, comments that this is "certainly an age of anxiety" and that "most of us will have to admit that we live out our lives on an ocean of fear." Our cultivation of moment-to-moment awareness through mindfulness leads us to notice much sooner when feelings of fear are arising within us; we can take our attention to the breath and start to examine the perceived threat from a place of intense, kindly curiosity and zoomed-out perspective. Ultimately we can short-circuit the stress response and cause the parasympathetic nervous system to be activated.

Case Study: Peter (aged 12)

In our time of working together, it became clear that watching the daily news with his parents was a source of many of Peter's anxieties and putting his amygdala on constant high alert. He would become very anxious if he wasn't with his mother, telling me, "So many bad things happen in the world that I'm terrified something will happen to Mum when I'm not with her." We explored how fear feels in the body and Peter became able to recognise earlier on when he was becoming anxious so that he could bring his attention to his breath and notice the stories that his mind was telling him. We talked of how it feels to not be able to control the external world, but how we might have choices about our internal environment and how we choose to relate to what is happening. We also used visualisation along with breathing techniques so that Peter could learn ways to activate his parasympathetic nervous system and calm his amygdala. He decided to stop watching the news and asked his parents to fill him in on any world events that they thought he should know about.

As adults practising mindfulness, we become more present, calmer, more patient, kinder, less judgmental and more accepting; all of this creates a household or classroom with a very different energy, and out of this beautiful energy something quite miraculous begins to awaken!

6

Mindfulness, Meditation, Visualisation and Insight

"The Butterfly"
I chase her precious beauty – so fragile, pure and free!
I long to hold her gently, why won't she come to me?

Running through the meadow, I reach an old oak tree,
I pause to catch my breath, and suddenly I see...

What I seek was never lost, was never mine to gain.
My endless search for things outside me causes me the pain.

Her beauty is inside of me, and now I've stopped the search,
she's on my shoulder quietly – my body is her perch.
Heather Grace MacKenzie

So we've looked a little at what mindfulness is, and by now, having tried out the practices (or 'meditations') outlined in the book so far, you've begun to experience mindfulness for yourself. Perhaps you've realised that we already know how to pay attention to something, and indeed we do – we're just not very good at it! Do the phrases 'butterfly-mind' or 'monkey-mind' sound like they could describe you? My head certainly feels like there's a troop of chattering monkeys in there sometimes, although thankfully that's much rarer now since starting on the journey of mindfulness. The poem above points to an essential aspect of mindfulness – it teaches us nothing new but rather it helps us to uncover what was there all along – the breathtakingly beautiful essence at the core of each of us that transcends the physical form we temporarily take. Mindfulness gives us a loving perspective on the ego and its desperate fight for survival, its survival dependent of course on the illusion of separation and on mental positioning – being 'right' while others are wrong, being 'more' while others are less, being 'better' while others are worse. Mindfulness helps us to peel away the layers of patterning, habitual tendencies and unhelpful behaviour, and also begins to reveal our underlying assumptions and expectations, so that we can really get to the heart of who we are and sense the ultimate connectedness of *all* things. Some say that a better word for what mindfulness points to is 'heartfulness'. Indeed, the Chinese symbol for mindfulness is directly translated as 'mind with heart', capturing a meaning that may resonate with you more deeply than the word 'mindfulness'.

The origins of mindfulness

Thirty or so years ago, a man called Jon Kabat-Zinn along with some of his peers at the University of Massachusetts began exploring extracting the secular wisdom of the Buddhist teachings, what we term as 'mindfulness', and teaching this in a therapeutic environment to groups of individuals who were experiencing chronic health difficulties. What transpired was, in my view, nothing short of miraculous and has contributed in no small part to this time of momentous change in the collective consciousness. The ancient root of mindfulness in Buddhism is *sati* – mental qualities of awareness, attention and remembering (who we truly are). The adoption of mindfulness by Western psychotherapy has caused some additional qualities to be included that are beyond *sati*: qualities that include non-judgement, acceptance and compassion. These additional qualities are implicit in Buddhist teachings but it has been, and continues to be, very helpful to make them explicit when teaching mindfulness in a secular way, otherwise we would be stripping away the heart of what enables mindfulness training to make such a huge difference in people's lives.

Jon Kabat-Zinn famously defines mindfulness as "the awareness that emerges through paying attention on purpose, in the present moment, and nonjudgmentally to the unfolding of experience moment to moment." Other names for therapeutic mindfulness include 'affectionate awareness', 'mindful acceptance', 'open-hearted presence', and 'mindful compassion'. The word, "nonjudgmentally" doesn't imply that we should learn to never judge – we make judgements all the time and much of this is necessary for our survival – but it does mean that we learn not to get caught up and swept away by our judgements. We develop the ability to maintain our perspective much more easily, as if remembering we're watching our life play out like a movie and we're sitting in a seat at the cinema with a nice big box of popcorn (or other inspirational movie snack).

Throughout most of our daily lives we are preoccupied with thoughts of the future (planning, worrying) or thoughts of the past (analysing, ruminating) and living much of our lives on automatic pilot. Have you ever driven from A to B and arrived at B without any recollection of the journey? This is not at all uncommon and is a perfect example of automatic pilot in action. Mindfulness involves switching off automatic pilot and redirecting our attention back to the present moment, kindly, patiently and firmly, every time we notice it has wandered away from the present moment and become lost in thinking, and it also involves cultivating an attitude that is kind, patient and allowing.

One of the biggest misconceptions is that mindfulness is about stopping our thoughts or 'emptying the mind' or about relaxation. We do start to realise that our thoughts are the cause of our suffering, and that much of the time our mind is generating thoughts relating to the past or the future (or if related to the present moment then our thoughts are mostly concerned with judging this moment – is it satisfactory, unsatisfactory or neutral?) but, based on the principle of *what we resist persists*, it is profoundly unhelpful to try to push away our thoughts or to make our minds become quieter or stiller. *Trying* to empty the mind will usually have quite the opposite effect! Generally, our mindfulness practice *does* lead to a quieter and more spacious mind, and we tend to feel more relaxed because we learn to tend to the body kindly and we're no longer so caught up in the persistent cycles of worry and rumination, and all of this is because we don't try to stop our thoughts – we simply allow them to arise and learn to leave them alone, as best we can, rather than engaging with them.

Essentially, mindfulness is about developing a particular kind of awareness, an awareness that is full of heart, warmth and acceptance of whatever thoughts, emotions and body sensations are arising in each moment. We become the compassionate observer of our experience, grounding and rooting ourselves into *this* moment so that we can truly be alive, opening our hearts and our senses to *allow life to live through us*. We may notice the tender shoots of the first snowdrops poking out of the ground on a crisp January morning as we leave home in the morning, and the proud puffed-out red breast of the rather rotund little robin perching on the branch of the larch tree nearby, instead of being consumed by thoughts of the stressful moments recently experienced in the rush to get the children up, dressed, breakfasted and ready for school, or thoughts of the day ahead – work, deadlines, after-school activities, homework, supper.

What is meditation and what does it have to do with mindfulness?

When explaining meditation to children and teens, I often ask whether they have been taught that exercise is good for the body. Usually there's plenty of nodding, and I then go on to say that we can think of meditation as mind-exercise. Just as physical exercise keeps the body healthy, meditation keeps the mind healthy. We then go on to discuss and dispel any myths that centre around meditation needing to involve (a) sitting in the lotus position; (b) having the hands in certain mudras (positions); (c) chanting; and (d) a serene expression on the face!

When we refer to meditation in the West, we are generally talking about a formal practice that involves sitting on a chair or a cushion (or sometimes lying down). Mindfulness meditation is a particular kind of meditation that involves inviting the mind, in a kind and patient way, to come back to the present moment each time we notice it has wandered off into thinking. There are many other forms of meditation, including mantra meditation, Transcendental Meditation (TM), chakra meditation, third-eye meditation, zazen (Zen) meditation, vipassana (insight and wisdom) meditation, metta (loving-kindness) meditation, gazing meditation and Kundalini meditation. In addition, each religious tradition has its own contemplative practice. The practices in this book contain a mixture of many different styles of meditation, with a strong emphasis on mindfulness. By including a wide variety of different types of practices, you can choose to share with your child those that you feel were most suited to your child's needs and their particular age, stage and personality. For example, an anxious and/or fidgety 4-year-old would most likely not be interested in the 4.1 Breath Awareness Practice but would perhaps enjoy the 16.1 Eskimo Kisses Practice that combines awareness of breath with the sense of touch and is more playful.

Eckhart Tolle in his audiobook entitled *What is Meditation?* describes meditation as "an alignment with the totality, without needing to mentally understand anything." Whilst perhaps a little nebulous, these words point to a letting go of the normal logical 'left-brained' way of trying to analyse and process our experience. Furthermore, he tells us: "Be present with the totality of your being. Our meditation is to be present with every cell of the body." This idea of being present with every cell of the body signposts us towards the sense of the aliveness that it is possible to feel when we invite the mind to drop into the body rather than whirring around like a hamster-on-a-wheel in the head. Essentially our meditation is *a focused practice of being mindful.* Tolle suggests that when we fully awaken our whole life becomes a meditation – there is no difference or separation between 'normal daily life' and 'meditation practice'. However, on our journey of awakening we will need to get used to setting aside a portion of our day to sit quietly and practise *being* rather than *doing.* The more we do this, the more our daily lives become infused with the qualities of mindfulness.

6.1 Exercise: Exploring Meditation Together

Find somewhere quiet, warm and comfortable to sit with your child and endeavour to cue in some way that this time spent together is a little different – perhaps you could sit together on some cushions on the floor and/or light a candle.

Spend some time together gently sharing thoughts about what meditation is – first of all ask your child what they think meditation is, acknowledging and thanking them for what they've shared, and then openly share your own thoughts. You may wish to explain that you've been learning a little more about meditation, and in particular a type of practice called 'mindfulness' and would be interested in learning more, along with your child. Explore how your child feels about this, and answer any questions that they might have, as best you can.

Aim to close this time together with a shared intention to embark on a journey of exploring meditation (and in particular, mindfulness meditation) with an attitude of curiosity and patience, and to help each other on this journey.

Tip: if you have a teen, you are more likely to simply sit and have a conversation with them about whether they've heard about mindfulness. We can encourage connection with a wish to become more mindful by sharing some of our own experience of how tricky our mind is. We might say something like, "I don't know about you, but my mind is hardly ever in the here-and-now, it's mostly in the past or the future. I'm either busy analysing how I *should* have done something or said something differently, or busy imagining some horrible outcome to a task or situation that I know is awaiting me. So I've been learning a little about this mindfulness stuff, and it kind of makes sense to me – we keep bringing our mind back to the present moment, every time we notice it's wandered off, and we learn to be really curious about our experience as well as patient and kind with ourselves. Apparently loads of top sportsmen and women use mindfulness to enhance their performance, and there's research that shows mindfulness is stonkingly good at helping people to feel happier in their lives! Would you be interested in learning a little more about this?"

Depending on their answer, you might then offer to purchase a book on the subject and/or a meditation CD for them – there are some recommendations in Appendix B. Even if the answer is a "no", this doesn't mean that learning mindfulness for yourself can't make a huge impact on your household and indeed on your teen. When we watch transformation in those we love, including greater presence, acceptance and an ability to hold space for difficult feelings, we can't help but be transformed ourselves. Each of us has the power to effect change in all that we see around us.

Where does visualisation come in?
Visualisation fits rather well with adoption of the expanded form of mindfulness in the West that explicitly includes compassion. Whereas mindfulness allows us to still the mind, visualisation activates the mind, body and heart in a way that allows us to actualise our potential. Imagery is powerful stuff, and doesn't

necessarily require us to have an actual image in our mind's eye – many people are not particularly visual but are able to have a 'felt sense' of the scenario that's being suggested. I believe that mindfulness and visualisation are equally important and it's perfectly possible to combine elements of the two in a meditation, but visualisation is particularly important for activating and opening the heart energy centre. The 4.2 Self-Compassionate Intention practice is an example of using visualisation to work with the energy of the heart. Here is another quite different visualisation to try:

6.2 Exercise: Shower of Light Visualisation*

Find somewhere comfortable to practise where you're unlikely to be disturbed.

Perhaps beginning by taking your attention to the toes first of all, noting what sensations are there to be noticed in this moment, and then expanding the awareness to include the soles of the feet, the sides of the feet, the tops of the feet and the heel, then slowly scanning upwards through the body.

As you move your attention upwards through the body, you may find that your attention moves more easily through some parts of the body than others. Nothing wrong with that, just noticing if that's the case. Remaining present, patient and kind if some areas of the body feel a little 'stickier' to move through than others. Kindly and gently allowing your attention to infuse each cell of your body.

When you reach the top of the head, resting the attention there for a moment. Perhaps imagining or having a felt sense now that you're standing underneath a shower of light. Instead of falling down around the body, like water would do, the light from this shower actually falls through the body, passing through each and every cell, awakening, illuminating and bringing balance. Maybe you become aware that the light has a particular colour, or perhaps it's a mixture of colours? Perhaps the light is even changing colour as it passes through the body! Or perhaps you just have a felt sense of this light moving through the body. Follow the flow of light down through the body, noticing any sensations as you do so, and pausing for a few breaths as your attention reaches the chest area and then continuing to take the attention down through the body. Perhaps there are sensations of tingling or buzzing, or of warmth or coolness, or maybe no sensations at all in certain areas.

When you reach the feet, you can visualise allowing the light to travel down through the soles of the feet and into the ground (if that feels OK), noticing any sense of connection with the earth beneath.

Finishing perhaps with a moment of gratitude for the constant unconditional support of the ground beneath us and setting the intention to allow our light to shine as brightly as it is destined to do, so that we may start to really fulfil our potential.

Perhaps one of the most challenging aspects of our practice is becoming aware of our fears and turning towards them rather than running away from them or pretending that they don't exist, which are by far the most common approaches to fear. Visualisation can be a particularly powerful antidote to fear. Are you living the life that you dream of? If not, what's holding you back? You may come up with all sorts of practical reasons why your life isn't currently fulfilling in every way that you'd like it to be (not enough money and/or not enough time are the two most common), but presence, joy, light, love and abundance are here *right now* for you if you choose them, and what holds us back always boils down to fear. I nearly didn't write this book. A little voice inside me said, "Who the hell do you think you are, thinking that you've got anything important to say?!" For a while I believed that voice, in spite of constant nudges by the Universe to write (angel cards telling me to write, clients asking me to put my thoughts down on paper, e-mails 'out of the blue' about writing courses). Then, one rainy study day, one of my university tutors read Marianne Williamson's poem entitled "Our Greatest Fear" to us. That day I smiled at the little voice inside me and sent her love; she was misguided, for each of us has something important to say.

"Our Greatest Fear"
Our greatest fear is not that we are inadequate,
but that we are powerful beyond measure.

It is our light, not our darkness, that frightens us.
We ask ourselves, who am I to be brilliant,
gorgeous, handsome, talented and fabulous?

Actually, who are you not to be?
You are a child of God.

Your playing small does not serve the world.
There is nothing enlightened about shrinking
so that other people won't feel insecure around you.

We were born to make manifest the glory of God within us.
It is not just in some; it is in everyone.

And, as we let our own light shine, we consciously give
other people permission to do the same.
As we are liberated from our fear,
our presence automatically liberates others.
Marianne Williamson

What is the relationship between mindfulness and compassion?

I mentioned earlier that we might see mindfulness and compassion as the two wings of a bird, and this is perhaps firstly because they are both equally necessary for the bird to fly, and secondly because the bird is a potent symbol of freedom. This freedom is liberation from mind-states that keep us trapped in our suffering (our internal resistance to what *is*). Practising mindfulness enables us to create a stability and clarity of mind, an ability to direct the torchlight of our attention and sustain our focus in a non-judgmental way. Building our compassion, through meditative practices designed to do just that, builds our inner resources so that we can not only notice our difficult thoughts, emotions, moods and mind-states (and those of others around us), but we can turn towards them with a commitment and energy directed towards alleviating the suffering that we see.

The more we practise mindfulness and compassion, the more we become aware of the extent to which we've been buying into stories, stories of *me* and who I think I am, and how other people are (or are not) meeting my needs. We begin to see what is arising for what it really is – part of the illusion of a permanent sense of self that is at the centre of the Universe. It's important not to underestimate the size of the task – this is difficult and uncomfortable work – and so it's really helpful to learn to go gently with ourselves and have a strong and well-tended intention to become deeply self-compassionate. The ego feels so very threatened by a reminder of its impermanence and the fundamental difficulty of life – the fact that each of us has a physical body that one day must return to the earth. And yet it is the facing of this difficult truth and the development of a deeper sense of something within us that is eternal that will set us free and that will set our children free. In order to evolve as human beings, we have to learn to turn towards our demons rather than run away from them or pretend that they don't exist, and (even more challenging than that) we must eventually face them with warmth, curiosity and compassion.

Insight – those moments of 'clear-seeing'

Mindfulness meditation as we know it in the West contains a strong element of insight training. As we get comfortable with becoming the observer of our experience, watching the thoughts, emotions and physical sensations pass through us, we can *turn our attention towards the observer* and notice the attitude of the observer. Is our observer a kind and compassionate one, or a harsh and critical one? What kind of assumptions and expectations or 'programs' is your observer running? In her extraordinary book *E-Squared: Nine Do-It-Yourself Energy Experiments That Prove Your Thoughts Create Your Reality*, Pam Grout points out that it is now known that the brain receives around *400 billion pieces of information per second* but it can only deal with around *2,000 pieces of information per second*. So the mind has to do some screening (cue extremely problematic tendency to suppress anything that doesn't fit with our current worldview), and discards 99.9995%, choosing only 0.0005% to work with! This screening is done by the unconscious mind which has been conditioned by the past and whose workings are not, on the whole, accessible to us except through our dreams and meditation. Neuroscientists tell us that around 95% of our thoughts are generated by the unconscious mind that has been conditioned by events of the past. So essentially our thoughts are simply echoes of the past that we buy into. How often do we actually remind ourselves that our thoughts are simply movements of energy, and not (in fact) fact?!

"My son shouldn't be behaving in this way." Fact? Who says so? As we begin to question our thoughts, we start to see that much of what we perceive is not real – our thoughts, emotions, moods and mind-states are very often a product of the past: our conditioning and our unresolved psychology. Through the field of social neuroscience, we are starting to become aware of the power of the unconscious and how much of our behaviour is driven by it.

So there's a kind of undercurrent of thoughts, attitudes and assumptions that's flowing along at a level that is below our conscious awareness and there's a part of the unconscious mind that is filtering this undercurrent based on assumptions, generalisations and also ancestral experience, but because it operates in the subliminal, for the most part we are unaware of what it's doing and yet our actions, moods and mind-states are a result of the activity! We think that we're in control of our actions and perceiving the world with clarity and logic, but actually on the whole our experience of life has very little to do with what's actually happening in the present moment! We are literally *seeing what we believe*, rather than the other way round. Teens can be surprisingly receptive to this information – my eldest (who was fourteen at the time) absolutely loved reading Pam Grout's *E-Squared* book and trying out the energy experiments, and I had a sense that he felt he'd discovered the magic of discovering that he is truly the master of his own destiny, with many more choices available to him than he'd ever imagined. This detail may be too much to share with a child, particularly when starting out sharing mindfulness with them, but it feels important to lay bare some of the complexities of our mindfulness practice so that it's apparent that this really is the journey of a lifetime and 'becoming mindful' isn't a checkbox that you can tick – it's not a destination! In the words of Edward Monkton in his *Zen Dog* cartoon: "He knows not where he's going, for the ocean will decide, it's not the destination, it's the glory of the ride."

7

Benefits of Meditation

It is never too late to turn on the light. Your ability to break an unhealthy habit or turn off an old tape doesn't depend on how long it has been running; a shift in perspective doesn't depend on how long you've held on to the old view. When you flip the switch, it doesn't matter whether it's been dark for ten minutes, ten years or ten decades. The light still illuminates the room and banishes the murkiness, letting you see the things you couldn't see before. It's never too late to take a moment to look.
Sharon Salzberg

You will most likely already be sold on the benefits of meditation if you have your own meditation practice or have dabbled a little with meditation in the past. When we experience meditation there is a deep knowing that it's doing us a power of good even if we don't know the physiology of what's actually happening. Whenever I teach the Connected Kids™ training courses and go through the benefits of meditation with a new group of students I am always filled with a renewed sense of awe – awe that we can actually change our brain and help ourselves in so many ways in a relatively short period of time by doing something as simple as practising *being* rather than doing.

The weight of research into the benefits of mindfulness meditation for adults is extraordinarily compelling, and emerging research into the benefits of mindfulness for children shows what it seems logical to assume – that the benefits for children are much the same as for adults. The Mindfulness in Schools Project's (MiSP) website has up-to-date information on the latest research available into the effects of mindfulness for children at http://mindfulnessinschools.org/research/research-evidence-mindfulness-young-people-general/.

I won't list individual research articles here as the information will be quickly out-of-date given the amount of research that's underway, but will broadly summarise how mindfulness can help you and your child. Google Scholar is an excellent research tool if you want to check out some of the latest research for yourself. It seems that there's very little that mindfulness *can't* help you with (OK, it can't help you put the kettle on, but it *can* help you to feel more comfortable with your thirst for a cuppa!).

What does the available research show?

Practising mindfulness is associated with the benefits listed below.

Improved quality of sleep – practising mindfulness means that our minds are less likely to be hijacked by worrisome thoughts at bedtime. It becomes easier to fall asleep, and sleep is less fitful and more restorative. Mindfulness is even helpful for those with insomnia and other sleep disturbances.

Reduced perception of stress – those who practise mindfulness feel less stressed and feel better able to cope with life's ups and downs.

Reduced physical symptoms of stress – breathing becomes deeper and so the cells of the body are better oxygenated, blood pressure is lowered, levels of inflammation in the body are reduced, immune function improves. Regular meditators are admitted to hospital far less often for cancer, heart disease and numerous infectious diseases.

Reduced anxiety – we become better able to be with uncertainty in our lives, and actually may come to embrace uncertainty, noticing that it brings with it a sense of aliveness. We learn to approach fears in a curious and kind way.

Reduced depression – research points to mindfulness meditation helping to reduce likelihood of relapsing into further episodes of depression through (1) creating space around triggering events to allow a more considered response rather than unconscious reaction; (2) facing of fears; and (3) learning to be present for others, resulting in improved relationships. Research shows that mindfulness meditation is at least as effective as drugs or counselling for the treatment of clinical-level depression.

Greater emotional regulation and emotional intelligence – we become much more in touch with the emotions passing through us and can experience these from a sense of greater perspective, allowing us to get less 'caught up' in what is arising. Experts refer to this as 'emotional regulation', but actually we're not controlling our emotions as such, we're just better able to experience fully what is arising and to allow it to be *just as it is* without getting so heavily pulled into the maelstrom. We can more easily detect and identify the emotions arising in others, without judgement.

Increased sense of well-being and improved mood – a great many studies have reported the positive impact of mindfulness on a general sense of well-being and mood. Meditating really does make us feel happier and have a much more positive outlook!

Increased self-esteem – it has been shown that mindfulness is very beneficial for those with low self-esteem (which is all of us, from time to time). Learning to bring self-compassion to our human predicament allows us to stop beating ourselves up when we don't feel or perform as we think we should. It's a common misconception that being hard on ourselves motivates us and keeps us on our toes – keeps us on track to do well in life – and that self-compassion is 'soft'. Actually it's quite the opposite. Research shows that self-compassionate people are just as motivated as self-critical people, but are far more likely to keep trying if they fail at something, and are far more likely to make healthier choices for themselves when it comes to food and exercise etc.

Better ability to focus and sustain attention – we choose the object of our focus and we return our minds, over and over again, to the present moment. This very act strengthens our ability to direct our attention wherever we choose and to remain focused.

Enhanced quality of relationships – we learn to bring presence to our interactions with others. We remain present to our own needs whilst also being sensitive to the needs of others (expressed through both verbal cues and body language). We are less reactive and less identified with stories of our past and a need to be right. We are better able to see situations from a 'zoomed-out' perspective.

Increased resilience – we constantly seek to control the outer circumstances of our lives, and yet this endeavour can never be truly successful as the one constant in life is change, and life is in charge of this, not us. Mindfulness brings with it a compassion that allows us to hold the difficulties we experience in a tender embrace, like a mother holding a newborn child. As we learn to flow with life rather than resist it, we can really get in touch with a sense of aliveness that comes from being in alignment with life, even if the circumstances of our lives are not comfortable or easy. We learn to weather life's storms like a well-equipped ship with a sturdy anchor.

Reduced pain – mindfulness can significantly reduce perceived pain levels and the emotional reaction to pain. Many studies have shown that substantial reductions in pain levels can be achieved after only a few weeks of practising meditation.

Improved memory – mindfulness improves working memory, the short-term 'workspace' memory that we use when doing things such as mental arithmetic or following spoken directions.

Enhanced creativity – the brains of regular meditators have been shown to be much less cognitively rigid (i.e. are freer to come up with ideas) than non-meditators. Cognitive rigidity is to do with how flexible your brain is in solving problems. Non-meditators tend to be 'blinded' by past experience whereas meditators are used to holding their thoughts in a non-judgmental open field of awareness which means they are less likely to overlook novel and adaptive ways to solving the problem.

I hope I've given you more than enough reasons to fuel your motivation to practise mindfulness. It's worth mentioning here that guided imagery, sometimes referred to as GIM and also known as guided visualisation, confers many similar benefits to mindfulness meditation. Many studies have demonstrated improved immune function, faster recovery times after surgical interventions, better tolerance of chemotherapy in terms of both mood and symptoms experienced, reduced levels of depression, anxiety and fatigue, and reduced levels of pain. It is often combined with progressive muscle relaxation, which I give an example of later on.

8

Method – the 'How'

Meditation practice isn't about trying to throw ourselves away and become something better, it's about befriending who we are.
Ani Pema Chödrön

In the previous chapter we looked at the 'why' of meditation. In this chapter we explore *how* we actually learn mindfulness and I will attempt to address many of the 'frequently asked questions' that participants of mindfulness courses tend to ask. It's really worthwhile getting an overview of the basics right at the beginning, if you're new to meditation. I'm going to set out the stages of mindfulness meditation practice in the way that the Mindfulness Association (www.mindfulnessassociation.net) teaches, because I think it's a really helpful way of structuring things, and explain why each of these steps is useful. It's a little like learning to drive a car – when we've been driving for a while we don't need to think about putting our seatbelt on, sinking the clutch, starting the ignition, selecting a gear etc., it just all happens automatically. The same is true for mindfulness meditation – after we've been doing it for a little while the steps become second nature, but if we're aware of the steps then we have a basis of knowledge, as well as experience, from which to guide a child so that we can lead practices that will help to settle their mind, bring them into their body, and help them to explore their inner landscape. Understanding the 'how' of meditation really sets the foundation for then approaching the 'what'.

Before we begin looking in more detail at the 'how' of meditation, let's take a closer look at what we're working with – this disobedient mind!

8.1 Exercise: Purple Feathers

Sitting quietly and reading through the exercise and then allowing the eyes to close for a couple of minutes.

Wherever you find yourself, in this moment, simply decide to close your eyes for a couple of minutes and give your mind a complete rest. Deciding to do absolutely nothing, not even think. Allow your mind to have a complete rest and put its feet up (so to speak). In particular, not thinking about purple feathers, or the kind of animal or bird that might have purple feathers.

Resting here with the firm intention of doing absolutely nothing, not even thinking.
Allowing this mind to have some time off from 'doing', including thinking, and particularly not thinking about a purple feather or bringing to mind an image of a purple feather.

What happened in the above exercise? Did your mind listen to your request for it to just rest, or did something else happen – perhaps the mind just couldn't resist fetching an image of a purple feather, or perhaps there were thoughts about what a bird with purple feathers would look like. If your mind felt empty of thought, but the exercise felt a bit effortful (perhaps noticing a tension in the brow or some sense of clamping down somewhere in the body), it's possible that you managed to suppress thinking for the moments of the practice. This isn't a strategy that will get us very far though – we can suppress thoughts and emotions for a short while, but (a) it's pretty exhausting and (b) it's rather like wearing support-pants, i.e. whatever you clamp down on and stuff inside has to come out somewhere! When we suppress emotions, they stay locked in the body until an event triggers an often alarmingly-forceful outpouring; this is often quite dispro-portionate to the triggering event.

So we've perhaps learned from the previous exercise that the mind 'has a mind of its own' in that it doesn't tend to do what we tell it to do. We can intend to do nothing, but lo-and-behold images, thoughts, memories, storylines and feelings all arise in spite of our intention. This is our starting point, and the good news is that scientists now know that the mind is very trainable. Previously it was thought that an adult mind was fairly fixed in its structure and function, but we now know that an adult mind it is still very adaptable (this is known as neuroplasticity) and scientists have observed significant changes in the physical structure of the brain after an 8-week mindfulness course.

Environment

If possible, have a space that is set aside for your practice and that you can return to without having to set it up each time. I like to think of my tiny little meditation room as my *heart cave* and I've painted it a deep red and decorated it with items that are meaningful to me – some pictures of my family, crystals, a crystal lotus flower candleholder that I use when teaching Reiki, a nice little rug, my meditation cushions (with spare under my altar table in case any of my children wish to join me) and a couple of soft blankets. Whether you have a room that you can set aside for your practice or not, decorate the space in which you meditate with a few select items that help you to get in touch with and to open your heart. When we create a space that reflects what we love, the heart naturally opens and feelings of loving-kindness flow much more easily, both to others and to ourselves.

When creating a meditation space for a child, it's a lovely idea to have the child (or children) make a sign for the door to let others know that there's meditation going on. For example, younger children may enjoy a 'Ssshhhh, quiet time in progress' sign, or a picture of Zen Dog meditating or something similar. Older children may prefer a 'Please don't interrupt' sign. Children tend to feel a sense of importance to the occasion when a candle is lit, and I've been surprised that in every school I've taught I've been allowed to light a candle for our sessions. In a relatively harsh school environment, with glaring lighting and generally devoid of soft furnishings, putting overhead lights off, closing blinds a little and lighting a candle can powerfully signal a change in tempo, moving from *doing* mode to *being* mode.

Posture

The next piece of the jigsaw puzzle to put in place when we are learning to meditate is learning to place the body during our practice in such a way that the posture reflects SHAIDS:

- Secure base – Weeble-like position
- Honouring the body – this amazing body that's always moving towards balance
- Alignment – with life
- Importance – of the practice
- Dignity
- Strength with softness – strong back, soft front

An awareness of our posture and how we hold ourselves in general can make a big difference to how we feel about ourselves and how we interact with others. A strong and dignified posture will help us to feel more confident, happier to assert our right to take up space in this world – our right to exist. My previous years of meditation practice had interestingly resulted in a good posture primarily *only* during meditation practice and not in daily life; my mindfulness practice has moved awareness of posture into daily life along with an awareness of how I *feel* about my posture. Holding a more erect and dignified posture, even when we don't feel like it, outside of our meditation practice also affects how we are perceived by others.

It doesn't matter whether you choose to make yourself comfortable with a meditation cushion on the floor or choose to sit on a chair to meditate – no position is more conducive to meditation than another, but it's helpful to refrain from lying down when practising unless it's the Body Scan practice or a visualisation. When we lie down it becomes harder to remain alert and aware of the thoughts, emotions and physical sensations arising within us. If sitting meditation is uncomfortable for you then by all means lie down – just set the intention to remain as alert as possible and if you find yourself dozing then that's what your body needed, no need to beat yourself up. If you notice yourself becoming a little sleepy during a practice and you've been practising with your eyes closed, you may find it useful to open your eyes for a moment – this tends to bring us back into a more alert state.

If you choose to sit on a chair, then it's helpful to sit a little forward from the back of the chair, at least at the start of the practice. Being self-supporting physically is a strong metaphor for being self-supporting in other ways and it sends a powerful message to the mind. As with posture on a meditation cushion, invite the spine to have its full length and to be tall and strong but not rigid. Allow that gentle inward curve in the lower back to remain, and tilt the chin downwards slightly so that the spine at the back of the neck has its full length. It may help to imagine a silken cord attached to the crown of the head that's gently pulling upwards to encourage the spine to lengthen a little, allowing each of the vertebra of the spine to have a little space. And we just sit with a strong spine, the rest of the body relaxed around this strong spine, shoulders rolled back a little so that the chest is nice and open, in this dignified position that reflects the importance of what we're doing – making a life for ourselves and for our child that involves an awful lot less suffering!

If using a meditation cushion (or two cushions, as I like to do) or meditation stool then all of the above applies, and the only difference really is that instead of sitting forward a little in the chair, we arrange ourselves on the cushion or stool so that the base of the spine is supported. I find it very helpful to use meditation cushions filled with buckwheat as this moulds to the shape of the body rather better than a kapok filling, and to arrange my body on the cushions such that my pelvis is pushed forward a little. My children enjoyed picking out their own meditation cushions immensely, choosing a colour that felt important to them and a size and shape that they liked.

When lying down for a practice such as the Body Scan (4.4 Body Scan) there are several different options for positioning. Many people lie flat on their back with their knees bent and with a cushion beneath the knees to support them. This takes some of the pressure off the lower back. Some prefer to lie face down (which may feel safer) or on their side, and there's really no wrong way to position the body. During the practice, it's really helpful to be mindful of tending to the needs of the body and if we become aware that the current position has become uncomfortable then we can bring some curious attention to the sensations of discomfort and then make a conscious choice regarding any change of position to bring more comfort and kindness to the body.

Intention and Motivation – what's important to you?

Once we've placed the body we can start to explore our intention and motivation for the practice, bringing a beginner's mind to this as best we can, in order to discern what feels real and true for us in the given moment. The intention sets the direction we want to travel in, whilst our motivation is the energy that propels us on our journey. Some meditators prefer to carry a relatively general intention, such as the intention to practise mindful awareness with an attitude of kindness and curiosity, whereas many meditators prefer to set an intention and explore motivation in relation to a particular practice. For example, my intention during a loving-kindness practice may be to explore the felt sense of loving-kindness and to soften my heart to myself and others.

My motivation for such a practice may be a wish to grow compassion for myself and others so that those around me may benefit from my capacity to hold my own difficulties and theirs in a more tender way and so that these benefits may ripple outwards to others in ever-increasing circles. Our intention and motivation may mature and change over time, so try to avoid any tendency to just bring to mind a well-rehearsed intention and motivation at the start of your practice by rote – see what feels right in that particular moment.

Settling the Mind

Once we're in a comfortable and supportive posture, and have set our intention and explored our motivation for a few moments, the next step is to begin to settle the mind. Exercise 4.1 Breath Awareness is a 'Settling the Mind' exercise. The 'Settling the Mind', 'Grounding', 'Resting' and 'Support' steps that are described here are known as 'SGRS' as taught by the Mindfulness Association. SGRS is a useful structure within which to frame our practice, particularly when we're guiding ourselves and/or a child.

The first thing to note when settling the mind is it's extremely helpful to let go of *trying* to do anything, least of all achieve a settled mind! It's paradoxical, I know, but the deepest truths generally are. We simply create the conditions to allow the mind to do what it naturally does – settle itself – when we leave our thoughts alone. We have, on the whole, developed the habit of continually stirring the pot, of shaking the snow globe, of continually engaging with the thoughts that arise if the thought has enough of a negative or a positive charge to it to suck us in to thinking. We can start to view our thoughts as clouds in the sky – we can just watch them go by. Thoughts arise, linger for a moment or two, then simply pass on by.

To choose not to engage with thought is much easier said than done, and when we begin practising mindfulness we will not notice the moment of choice to engage, we will simply notice that we've been thinking – often for a *long* time! Most helpful when we notice that we have been engaged in a train of thought is to hop off that train, returning again to the present moment, and be kind to ourselves rather than beating ourselves up for having become distracted (again)! Some mindfulness teachers use the analogy of exercising the mindfulness muscle every time we notice distraction and return our attention to the present moment, and the muscle becomes stronger each time we bring our attention back. In my own practice I've found this to be a really useful way to view things – there's a tendency for us to feel like our practice time has been worthless if we've spent our time almost entirely in distraction, but actually often after these kinds of practice I really notice a much greater sense of space in my daily life and realise that my time on the cushion (or on the chair) wasn't misspent at all.

When teaching a child how to settle their mind, it's a great idea to make a little snow globe to demonstrate how the mind spends most of its time all shaken up and how it can settle itself when we leave the thoughts alone.

8.2 Exercise: Make a Snow Globe

Find a clear sealable container such as a jam jar and raid your craft supplies for some glitter or small beads. Decide on the scene with your child – perhaps they enjoy Lego (which survives water very well) in which case you might create a small Lego scene at the bottom of your container. Plasticine also works well in water but can be quite buoyant depending on the shape that you create, so you may need to use some glue to hold it in place. If you do use glue to set the scene in place, please make sure the glue is dry before you add the glitter (or beads) and the water.

If you want to really go-to-town then you can get some glass paint

*and give your scene a backdrop! Once your snow globe is ready, you
can invite your child to give it a good shake and then perhaps ask
whether they can see how their mind might feel a little like a shaken-
up snow globe when it's full of thoughts. The very act of watching
the scene settle in the snow globe together is an opportunity for you
both to practise mindfulness, perhaps observing the flow of the
breath into and out of the body as the scene settles, and noticing how
dropping our attention into the body can help the mind to settle.*

*If you'd prefer to simply buy a snow globe, there are some lovely
fairy snow globes and Peter Pan snow globes available, rather than
the more traditional Christmas scenes that are obviously seasonal.*

The more we practise mindfulness, the fewer thoughts the mind
will tend to generate and the more spacious the mind will
perhaps start to feel, but when we seek this in our practice, we
doom ourselves to more suffering because we create a tension
between where we are and where we *want* to be. Resisting what
is fuels further thinking because we instantly move into thoughts
of judgement. I heard a wonderful quote the other day from a
mindfulness teacher who'd been teaching her daughter to
meditate. After a relatively short practice, the daughter had
turned to her mum and said, "Mummy, when my attention is in
my head it kind of feels like there's a really loud party going on
in there and it's quite hard work, but when my attention drops
down into my body then it's like being in a peaceful and quite
beautiful garden!" Well, 'out of the mouths of babes', as they say.
That's it – mindfulness in a nutshell – as taught to us by a 7-year-
old girl.

In this settling phase of our practice, we give the mind
something else to focus on, rather than thoughts, and because
our breath is always with us it's a useful anchor to come home to.
Invite the breathing to deepen very slightly, just for this settling
phase, and introduce counting if you find that helpful. Breathe in

whilst counting to 3 or 4, noticing any pause between the in-breath and the out-breath, breathe out to a count of 3 or 4, noticing any pause between the out-breath and the in-breath. So doing two things – breathing and counting – and if the mind wanders off, just bringing it back to the breathing and the counting. Then after a minute or two (or longer if the mind is very unsettled), letting go of the counting and allowing the breath to return to its natural rhythm and pace. Moving the attention now to the out-breath and any sense of relaxation in the body as the body releases the breath. Inviting the mind to learn from the body: body releases breath and relaxes a little, mind releases engagement with thinking, and begins to settle down. Allowing each in-breath to be a new beginning, and each out-breath a complete letting go of whatever is ready to be released.

Another good way of getting in contact with the breath is to place a hand or both hands over the belly and tune into the sensations of movement there. Children tend to really enjoy this, and it's a good way to help the mind to settle when lying quietly at bedtime, gently paying attention to the sensations of the movement of the breath in the body through the lens of touch – the strongest of our senses to hold us in the present moment.

For some people, the breath is a source of anxiety – particularly for those who have a health difficulty that affects breathing, such as asthma. If that's the case for you, or your child, then perhaps explore paying attention to the breath in a relaxed way and notice how it feels for you. If you start to notice any sense of tightening or tensing in the chest, shoulders or throat, or any feelings of resistance or shutting down to the experience, then you may find it helpful to move straight into the grounding phase of the practice and perhaps direct your attention initially to the lower half of the body, exploring sensations of contact and pressure there.

Grounding

Next, we move into Weeble mode, i.e. we direct our attention more fully into the body with the intention of having a secure base, of feeling mountain-like. We can begin by taking our attention first of all to the points of contact between the body and whatever it's resting on, noticing how gravity creates sensations of contact and pressure where parts of the body meet the chair, the bed, the cushion, the stool or the floor. What *exactly* do the sensations feel like that we label 'contact' and 'pressure'? As we invite our awareness into the whole of the body, we can imagine that we're scanning upwards through the body like a scanner, or we can rest in a more open awareness and allow the body to present different sensations to us in a more 'popcorn' kind of a way.

As we rest in the body, perhaps we're also aware of the subtler sensations of the clothing or jewellery resting against the body. Perhaps there are some strands of hair that are resting against the face or neck. We might become aware of the space around the body, and begin to realise that there's an awful lot of space around us – right out to the farthest reaches of the Universe – and noticing any tendency of the mind to open out, to expand, as we invite the mind to open out to the space around us. Once we have come home to this body of ours, with a sense of the body supported unconditionally by the ground beneath and perhaps also a sense of the body being willing and able to unconditionally support the mind as it rests, we can move into the resting phase. The settling and grounding phases are really setting the scene for the guts of the practice – exploring our inner world through resting in *being*.

Resting

Ah, resting. Even the word sounds nice, doesn't it?! Inviting the mind to rest in the support of the body, noticing how awareness of the body can hold the mind in the present moment. As we rest, we are in complete non-doing and surrender to (as Eckhart Tolle calls it) the *suchness* of this moment, i.e. we let go of resisting what *is*, because it's here anyway. So if we notice a contraction in the belly and a slight flush of the cheeks and realise that anger is here, well then anger's just what's here. We might prefer that it wasn't, but actively seeking a different state just puts the body in a state of resistance and creates further suffering. Anger's here, so we do our best to befriend it, get to know it, and intend to be kind to ourselves because it feels difficult. Our tendency whenever we find ourselves feeling a certain way is to try to analyse *why* we feel that way, but our practice invites us to stay present with the feeling without analysing. When we move into analysis then we are back in the head, and we spiral into a negative cycle of rumination and self-recrimination, or the ego will move quickly to establish and strengthen its position of being 'right', and in doing so making others 'wrong'.

In the state of resting, we allow our experience to unfold in each moment and we simply watch, with kindness and curiosity, what unfolds. Allowing a river of thoughts, images, storylines, emotions and physical sensations to arise, to play out, and to pass by in their own time. Our job is to sit on the riverbank, quietly watching, and to clamber back out of the river and on to the riverbank each time we notice we've dived into the river to engage with a thought that kind of sucked us in and dragged us along with it.

Particularly in the early stages of learning mindfulness, it's really helpful to make use of a support as we rest. We place a small portion of our attention very lightly, like a feather landing softly on a stream, on the sensations of breathing or the direct experience of sound in order to drop anchor into the present moment. Using a support means that we are less likely to drift off into thinking, and quicker to return to present-moment awareness when we do drift off.

Support – Mindfulness of Breath

The breath is one of the most powerful balancers and something that we can come home to in *each and every moment*. A microcosm of the cycle of life, our breath is with us from the moment we take our first breath until the moment we return home to Source. The 4.1 Breath Awareness exercise in Chapter 4, although short, is enough to press the 'reset' button to activate the parasympathetic nervous system.

Paying attention to the breath gives us a real insight into what's going on for us at any point in time. When I notice that my breath catches briefly, this often cues me to direct my attention to my thoughts where I will find a memory playing of a difficult moment in the past and I'm then aware that my mind has chosen to label the associated emotion as 'embarrassment' because my breath often catches when the discomfort of embarrassment is playing out. When there's a heavy sensation associated with my breathing, along with a slight ache in the chest area, I may be alerted to a sad feeling passing through me. These are wonderful opportunities to pause and set the intention to be kind to myself as this moment of difficulty passes through.

When leading children in breathing practices, we need to be aware that young children may become quite bored and restless if just paying attention to the relatively subtle sensations of the breath. Sometimes a few minutes of some vigorous movement, for example dancing madly as if no one's watching, is an outlet for high energy and enough to bring the child into a more embodied state for a few minutes of a breathing practice. Alternatively, you could incorporate some movement into the practice and suggest that this movement is synchronised with the breath. An example is given below in Exercise 8.3 Heart Breathing which most children (and some teens) will enjoy. If you'd like to extend the period of practice with your child and perhaps lead them in a visualisation, then settling and grounding is a great place to start before inviting the child to move into visualisation.

8.3 Exercise: Heart Breathing

Ask your child to touch index fingers together and their thumbs together to make a heart shape (you may need to demonstrate this to the child before the exercise) and then suggest that they may want to now bring the other fingers of the hands together until the tips of the fingers touch.

You can guide the practice along the lines of the following words:

Allow your eyes to close if that feels OK, so that you can really concentrate on tuning into your body. If you'd prefer to keep your eyes open, then relax the muscles around your eyes so that your gaze is soft and fuzzy and it might feel like you're looking out of the sides of your eyes.

When breathing out, bring the index fingers down to meet the thumbs; when breathing in, move the index fingers back out to make a heart shape again. Keep moving in time with the breath.

Alternative Support – Mindfulness of Sound

The qualities of sound have an ability to bring a sense of spaciousness to our experience – a perfect antidote to our incessant 'busyness'. If you're a worrier, then I would suggest that you use sound as your preferred support rather than breath. When we're prone to anxious thoughts then the superhighways of anxious thinking are well established in the brain and we tend to try to control our environment as much as possible; paying attention to the breath may in this case make us more anxious as it's one more thing to control or worry about! Sounds are much less predictable and it's much harder to control them. The great news is that if you do have 'anxiety superhighways' in your brain then the practice of mindfulness may well help them to turn into little goat-tracks over time.

We can pay attention to faraway sounds, perhaps outside of the room if you're indoors right now. We can pay attention to sounds that are closer, maybe in the room with us or just nearby, perhaps the ticking of a clock. We can begin to notice some of the very subtle sounds – sounds associated with swallowing, with our breathing, perhaps even noticing a sound associated with the blinking of our eyes! As well as the forms (the sounds), we can also choose to become aware of the silence *beneath* the sounds, paying close attention to what surrounds and underlies each sound. Words would be meaningless without space in between them, and yet in this world obsessed with *things* we rarely pay attention to non-things – space, silence, the formless out of which all things arise.

8.4 Exercise: Sound Awareness*

Find somewhere comfortable to practise. All noises are welcome in this practice and so it's helpful to find somewhere to practise where you know that there will be sounds to become aware of.

Beginning by setting the intention to be mindful of sound, and to allow sound to act as an anchor to the present moment, and then we'll spend a little time settling the mind as we did in the earlier practice, 4.1 Breath Awareness.

Beginning to tune in to the sensations of the breath as if you've never experienced breathing before and bringing a real attitude of curious exploration to this practice, as best you can.

Tuning in to the sensations of the in-breath, allowing the breath to be just as you find it.

Tuning in to the sensations of the out-breath, allowing the breath to be just as you find it.

Noticing any pause between the in-breath and the out-breath, and between the out-breath and in the in-breath.

Perhaps introducing counting now. Counting up to 3 or 4 on the in-breath and the same number of the out-breath, and doing that for a few breaths. So doing two things in this moment – breathing and counting, but only if you find the counting helpful.

If you start to become anxious or tense with the counting, then let the counting go and just focus on the sensations of the breath entering and leaving the body. Maybe you're aware of cool air rushing past the insides of the nostrils as you breathe in, maybe you can feel warm air rushing past the insides of the nostrils as you breathe out, or maybe the lips. Perhaps there are sensations of stretching in the belly with the in-breath, perhaps movement in the shoulders, the chest, the back.

Letting go of any counting now. Watching the tide of the breath. The tide rolls in... the tide turns... the tide rolls out... the tide turns. Riding the waves of the breath for a few moments.

Resting your attention on the out-breath now. How does it feel as the body lets go of the breath?

Noticing any tendency of the body to relax a little bit as it releases what it no longer has any need for, and inviting the mind to learn from that. Body releases the breath and relaxes a little bit, mind releases engagement with thinking, and begins to settle down. Reminding ourselves that the mind naturally knows how to settle; we just need to learn to stop stirring the pot and getting involved with our thoughts. Not trying to stop our thoughts, but just watching them pass on by like clouds in the sky.

Inviting the attention to inhabit the whole of the body now, aware first of all of the points of contact between the body and whatever it's resting on and noticing what sensations of contact and pressure actually feel like.

More generally, what physical sensations are here to be noticed in the body right now? How does your body feel in this moment? Maybe there's a general feeling-tone of tiredness or sluggishness, maybe the body feels quite energised, maybe the body feels quite achy or fidgety... maybe something else. Reminding ourselves that there's no wrong way to feel, just opening up to what's here, as best we can, with curiosity and warmth.

Becoming aware of the space around the body now; this breathing body, as it rests here. So much space... right out to the farthest reaches of the Universe. Tuning into the space around the body, and perhaps also finding some space within.

And within this space, we simply rest. Nothing to do right now. No role to play, nothing to achieve. Not even trying to meditate.

Sooner or later, we will find that we've become distracted – a juicy thought arose and the mind hopped on to a train of thought that may have taken us quite a long way down the track before we realised what was happening. Nothing wrong – this is just what minds do, and this is why we gently rest our attention now on the support of sound. So this 'gently' term simply means that we allow sounds to come to us, rather than seeking them out, and we don't hold so tightly on to sounds that we shut other aspects of our experience out. Thoughts, physical sensations and emotions will still arise in our experience, but we leave them alone (as best we can) as we tune into the soundscape all around and within.

This use of support is like a dance – sometimes we may feel the mind is quite busy and distracted, so we may rest more of our attention on sound; other times when the mind feels quite spacious and relaxed, we may rest a tiny proportion of our attention on sound and the remainder of our attention is open to whatever else is arising within our experience.

Paying attention to faraway sounds, and noticing any tendency of the mind to become more expansive as it does that – opening out.

Paying attention to closer sounds.

Perhaps even noticing the sounds of your own breathing or swallowing.

Seeing if you can let go of the need to label and categorise sound, and just allow the sound waves to reach your ears like a melody or simply as raw sound waves. Seeing if you can be with ALL sounds with the same attitude, letting go of 'like' and 'dislike' and allowing the sound to be just as it is.

Finishing by dedicating the benefits of your practice in whichever way feels appropriate – using your own words in your mind's eye to express what feels true for you in this moment.

Tip: you can deliver the above practice to an older child pretty much as it is. Younger children may really enjoy a practice that's pretty much the same but where you deliberately introduce a sound such as tuning forks, singing bowl or sansula (see Appendix B – Resources for Children). The 'travelling' quality of the sound from these instruments is quite captivating for many children, and you could even suggest that they allow the sound waves to pass through them, noticing how that feels, or that they imagine breathing in the sound and allow it to move through them.

When to Practise and How Long

Many meditation teachers will tell you that first thing in the morning is the best time to meditate, for the most part because the mind tends to be less shaken up first thing in the morning – a little more spacious and not fully invested yet in the 'to do' list for the day – but also because meditating in the morning can help to set the tone for the rest of the day. However, those of us who are parents have to find a way to bring meditation into what often already feels like an overwhelmingly full schedule. We may find ourselves being bounced upon in the a.m. by a very awake little person who has no intention of leaving mummy or daddy alone to have their quiet time! Perhaps the most helpful advice I can give is to set the intention to choose a regular time to meditate – it doesn't matter what time of day – and make best endeavours to stick to that, even if you only manage a few minutes before a family member (including a pet) is calling for your attention. We're forming new habits, and that takes some practice, so setting aside a regular time of the day is a great way to form the new habit of taking some time for ourselves, to nourish our souls and replenish the patience batteries. In my experience, children tend to prefer meditating when their energy is a little lower, for example after exercise or later in the day.

The question of "How long?" is a difficult question to answer. Most meditators meditate for somewhere between fifteen and forty-five minutes per day. When you first start practising, fifteen minutes can seem quite long enough, and indeed a bit challenging, but very soon we tend to find that we can sit for longer, but it's far more important to practise a little each day than to sit for three hours once a week, so don't get too caught up in worry about how long to practise for. Set the intention to practise daily, and don't beat yourself up if life gets in the way, just start practising again as soon as you can.

If, when you're practising, you find yourself wanting to stop – perhaps you've started to feel really fidgety and/or your mind is really trying to pull you back into *doing* mode – then bring your attention to whatever it is that's bothering you and tune into how it feels in the body, exploring the edge of your discomfort before making a conscious decision whether to end your practice there or not. Often the discomfort will pass when we bring a kind and accepting attention to it, although we don't take our attention there in order to make it go away, we bring our attention there because *it's there anyway* and we might as well be in helpful relationship with it rather than trying to push it away. We tend to react to most situations that arise in life before conscious thought has actually kicked in, and as a result we react out of our past conditioning rather than through present-moment awareness of what is true for us in that moment. Learning to explore the edge of our discomfort in our practice helps us to do this in daily life – we become responsive to situations rather than reactive.

If you're guiding yourself in your practice, then it's really useful to have a meditation timer handy so that your mind isn't agitated by thoughts of when to finish. You can use an app on your phone to do this, but make sure you can switch your phone on to airplane mode otherwise it is likely to distract you from practising. Many experienced meditators still use recordings to guide them in their practice, and there's nothing wrong with that at all – it's not more noble to guide yourself – and many will alternate guided practice with guiding themselves.

A rough guide for your child's practice is that they might manage around the same number of minutes per day as their age.

Sustaining Practice

One of the biggest barriers to keeping your meditation practice going will be your mind – yes, that old chestnut. Your mind will tell you that you're too busy to practise, and you will believe it. Remind yourself that actually you *create* time when you meditate.

Throughout my years of recent university study, my mind has continually tried to persuade me that I'm too busy to practise… I should just get on with my assignment right now and practise tomorrow. And then the same story the next day. But coming back to my intention – to practise mindful awareness and bring a curious, kind, patient, spacious and loving energy to my family and working life – reminds me to park my behind on my cushions and practise, because my behaviour and my attitude is completely different when I see myself as deserving of time to *be* rather than *do*. When I'm meditating daily, I can have one hundred things on my 'to do' list for the day and life still feels spacious. I am able to move through the day with clarity, focus and an inner peace that cannot be touched by normal external events. I am generally untroubled by the many different demands upon my attention, choosing where to place my focus and giving the task at hand my full attention until or unless something else more demanding of my attention arises. I say all of this not in a "Yay me, look how great I am at this mindfulness thing" kind of a way, but as in, "Hey, this is available for *all* of us, we just got out-of-touch with our hearts and started living in our heads."

Here are some of my top tips for remembering to practise:

- Create a habit of practising whenever you can, and be creative with your time. If you find yourself in a long queue at the supermarket checkout, then this is the perfect time to practise! Take your attention to your breathing, to the sensations in your body, to the sounds, the sights, the smells, the feeling of the shopping basket or trolley handle in your hand. Notice any feelings of impatience or frustration and see if you can simply allow them to be a part of your experience.
- Use mindfulness bells on your phone – there are loads of apps available and you can choose to have your phone

chime or vibrate at random moments through the day to remind you to be mindful.

- Put little notes around the house to remind you to be mindful – I particularly like my mindfulness fridge magnet that ensures I'm more mindful about my food choices (it steers me away from the ice cream, at least sometimes).

- Invest in a small vision board, or a 'vision scrapbook' where you pin up or paste inspirational words, photos or anything else that reminds you of your intention and what motivates you to become more mindful and compassionate. Keep this in a place where you can see it, often.

- Seek out other like-minded people to practise with and share experience with. The Mindfulness Association holds regular online sits that really help to create a sense of community, but it's also helpful to find a local meditation support group that you can attend.

- Get your child involved. Ask them what would help them to remember to come back to the present moment, with kindness. Perhaps they've drawn a picture after a meditation practice that you've done together, and they'd like this pinned up on their bedroom wall. Teens often enjoy using a subtle reminder such as small, round 'dot' stickers that they can attach to their mobile phone case, bedside table, school jotters, pencil case etc. Nobody else knows what they mean, but each time your teen sees one of these dots they are reminded to pause, breathe, and fully arrive into the present moment.

- Don't stress over it if you realised you've forgotten to practise or simply haven't managed to fit it in, just get back in the saddle. After all, this moment is a whole new moment, and this new moment is the perfect time to practise!

9

Attitude – the 'What'

True happiness is to enjoy the present, without anxious dependence upon the future, not to amuse ourselves with either hopes or fears but to rest satisfied with what we have, which is sufficient, for he that is so wants nothing. The greatest blessings of mankind are within us and within our reach. A wise man is content with his lot, whatever it may be, without wishing for what he has not.
Seneca

We've looked in relatively simple terms at the 'how' of meditating in the previous chapter, and also the 'why' through looking at the benefits of meditation. So let's now look at the 'what'. What do we intend for children (and indeed ourselves) to learn when we teach them mindfulness meditation and visualisation? Jon Kabat-Zinn lists seven attitudinal cornerstones (or 'pillars') of mindfulness: *beginner's mind, non-striving, non-judging, patience, trust, acceptance* and *letting go*.

To embody mindfulness means to have really integrated mindfulness and its attitudinal qualities into our way of being. When we embody mindfulness we really live these attitudinal qualities as best we can – they are not simply things we talk about, they infuse our actions and our interactions more and more as we continue with our mindfulness practice. Let's take a closer look at each of these qualities so that we can understand better their subtleties and how, when adopted together, they can light up the path from suffering to freedom.

I should probably say at this point that it's generally best not to talk to children about 'attitudinal pillars or foundations' – such folly will usually result in yawns, giggles or sniggers (understandably) and so I like to talk of the *seven guiding lights* that lead us to a happier, more joyful life. Children are often captivated by the deeper meanings behind those things that appear simple – we can suggest that seven is a pretty special number, and ask a child whether they can think of anywhere else in life that we see the number seven being significant. We can listen for answers and then suggest the seven notes on a musical scale, seven days of the week, seven colours of the rainbow, seven major energy centres in the body.

Guiding Light 1: Beginner's Mind

With a beginner's mind we let go of assumptions and generalising ('filling in the blanks') so that we can *really* be present and witness this moment fully. We switch off 'automatic pilot' and bring a kind, alert curiosity to our experience in each unfolding moment. There are many reasons for doing this, but for the most part our minds are in the habit of tuning out of the present moment so that they can wander off into the past (replaying past moments over and over again) or into the future (planning, analysing, predicting). Replaying the past does not result in new insights – new ways to understand a situation or to creatively solve a problem, and this is because the logical, analytical left brain that likes to problem-solve is not the place from where insights arise, so this habitual behaviour is generally a complete waste of time. Using fMRI scanners, scientists have shown that insights arise from the right side of the brain, and this is the side that we are more in touch with when we practise *being* rather than *doing*. The future, when it arrives as the present moment, is never as we feared or predicted it to be, and so worrying about how things will turn out is again a very unhelpful behaviour. Bringing our mind to the present moment, with automatic pilot switched off, allows us to tune into the moments of life that we will *never* capture again – what a tragedy it is that as a human race we are either on autopilot or only partially present for the majority of the moments of our lives!

I vividly recall a conversation with a friend who was recounting how she had 'shushed' her child so that she could hear the voice in her head – the thoughts that were playing out as a running commentary about the housework that needed to be done. It was the school holidays and the house was already pretty shipshape. Her 7-year-old daughter was tugging at her trouser leg, asking for a moment of attention. In that moment, with her daughter gazing up at her earnestly, there was an opportunity for connection, and my friend had a profound awakening as she found herself telling her daughter to be quiet so she could pay closer attention to her thoughts. Does this sound familiar? How often are we too stressed or too preoccupied to fully pay attention to this moment, and yet *this* moment is the only one that exists. The future never arrives as the future, only as the present moment.

Guiding Light 2: Non-striving

During our practice (our meditations) it's really helpful to let go of needing to be somewhere other than where we are. This is very tricky for Western minds given how much emphasis is placed on achievement and attainment of goals, but placing our minds on our goals for the future during our practice immediately causes a problem. We cannot be in the present while a portion of the mind is in the future. So during our meditations we do our best to remain unattached to any particular outcome and let go of the tension between where we are now and where we would like to be. We may embark on mindfulness practice to become less stressed, or kinder, or for some other reason related to our deepest well-being or that of those around us, but while we are practising it is best to let go of striving to be 'more' or 'less' of anything so that we can be fully present for what *is* in this moment. We can just do the practice without any expectations and then evaluate our 'progress' at a later stage, perhaps at the end of an 8-week course or after a longer period of practice.

This may sound paradoxical and indeed it is; wisdom traditions are full of paradoxes. We can come to feel the truth of such paradoxical notions with our whole being rather than our intellect. We will reach our goals not by trying to *change* the present during our practice but by being present with whatever arises.

Guiding Light 3: Non-judging

Most of our behaviour is driven by judgements that are made by the unconscious mind. We are minding our own business, resting in the present moment like the metaphorical observer sitting on the riverbank watching the river of thoughts, images, storylines, emotions and physical sensations flow by, when suddenly a moment of awareness alerts us to the fact that we've been absent, lost in a train of thought for quite some time – we were swimming along in the river. What happened? Judgement, that's what! The automatic habit that we have of judging *everything* we see and feel as good, bad or neutral is what gets us into trouble. Much of the time the judgement isn't objective at all – it's generally an unconscious snap judgement based on our fears, our past experience (not always a reliable way of relating to present-moment experience) and/or ancestral biases.

An attitude of non-judgement means that we train ourselves to become an impartial witness, watching how the mind labels, categorises and evaluates. By learning to observe the comings-and-goings of thoughts, emotions and sensations in our field of awareness with greater equanimity, and training ourselves to reside more in the present moment, we effectively 'zoom-out' and get a little more perspective; this means we have the space to respond rather than react. As our attitude of non-judgement begins to infuse our daily life, we tend to find that this space gives us the opportunity to *choose* how we respond to a situation, rather than reacting unconsciously.

Guiding Light 4: Patience

OK, this is the one that I have traditionally had a particularly hard time with. We would all love to be endlessly patient, but the reality of all the different aspects that each of us juggles in our lives means that we reach snapping-point all-too-quickly. We tend to find ourselves having the amount of patience that is proportionate to our energy levels, and also proportionate to the number of assumptions, expectations, 'shoulds' and 'shouldn'ts' that our minds are currently operating with. Practising patience during our meditations can really help us to practise patience in our daily lives when we notice things feel all-too-much or when we notice we are in a hurry for something to be different from how it is in this moment.

Practising patience – a form of wisdom in itself – means that we allow things to unfold in their own time. I have a powerful memory of being a young girl growing up on our farm and one morning watching a baby duckling weakly fighting its way out of its shell. I was keen to do the remaining work of peeling away the shell to free the duckling but my mother cautioned me by saying, "The duckling has its own journey, darling. As it pecks around in circles, the umbilical cord gets twisted and the blood supply becomes cut off. That means that the duckling won't bleed when the veins are broken as it hatches. Be patient." Practising patience returns us to an alignment with the flow of life rather than a state of resistance.

Guiding Light 5: Trust

I mentioned above the importance of trust in relation to patience, but trust goes even deeper than that. The process of learning to trust yourself and your feelings is at the very core of mindfulness, and will lead you to learn to *trust life itself*. Trust requires that we open our hearts, and in doing so we are vulnerable. And yet this is how it must be. Make decisions that *feel* right, even if they don't seem entirely logical. As you move along the path of life and come to a crossroads, choose the path that makes your heart sing. Always. Not just because I said so, but because you've learned to trust yourself to know what's right for you. Our mindfulness practice is a journey of learning to trust the wisdom of the body. You might tell a friend that you'd be happy to help her out doing some home baking for the school fair, but then feel a tightening in the pit of the stomach and realise that you've overcommitted yourself – you've got a million other things to do this week and your inability to say 'no' (kindly) has a habit of leading you to feel overwhelmed all-too-regularly. One of your friends might be gossiping about a mutual friend and you find yourself not necessarily joining in, but being complicit in what's transpiring by not disagreeing with any unkind words being spoken and by not removing yourself from the conversation; you become aware of an ache in your chest area and a tightening in your throat and in parts of your legs, alerting you to your body's wise wish to either speak up for your friend or to remove yourself from this situation. Trust your body, it'll keep you right!

Guiding Light 6: Acceptance

If we feel angry, and we'd rather feel happy, the only way to free ourselves from suffering is to say to ourselves, "OK, anger, I notice you're here, knocking at the door. Come on in. Let me really feel you then – let's get acquainted." We tune into the sensations of the body, noticing where the anger is being held, and stay present with it, softening around it. Most likely, when recognised, the energy will fade from the anger and it will go on its merry way whenever it's ready; we accept it not to make it go away but because it's here anyway, and so we might as well relate to it in the most helpful way which is to simply *allow it to be*. Nothing wrong with the anger. Nothing wrong with any emotion, it's just what we do with them. When we suppress our emotions, we are essentially pushing them down into a suitcase of pain that we carry around with us; Eckhart Tolle refers to this as "the pain body". Children (and many adults) often have a tendency to suppress emotion, not wishing to experience what is difficult or uncomfortable, but like a pair of support-pants, what you stuff down has to come out somewhere! This is why we are sometimes blindsided by a mercurial outburst from our child in what can seem like a dramatic overreaction to something relatively inconsequential. In such moments, when the child is in *full reactivity* (frequently called a 'tantrum', although we often associate this word with children, adults are equally as capable of being in full reactivity) a maelstrom of emotion has taken hold and logic takes a back seat. All we can do is stay present with the child, of course keeping them physically safe while the reactivity plays out, and we model non-resistance. If we become angry ourselves, we have moved into reactivity and feed the negativity that the child is currently in the grip of. In a state of acceptance, we are in alignment with the flow of life; we're not frantically paddling upstream against the rapids.

Guiding Light 7: Letting Go

This quality seems to me to be absolutely fundamental to freeing ourselves from suffering. We may notice that the mind finds it very hard to let go of some particularly juicy thoughts or feelings. An excellent example of this is when we feel that we've been 'wronged' in some way. Even experienced meditators may struggle with letting go from time-to-time, such is the power of our emotions. The ego, over and over again, tries to fuel our negative feelings towards the person who we perceive has wronged us and tries to justify our position as 'right' and theirs as 'wrong'. "They deliberately <insert any action here> to upset me. They should have known how much this would upset me. How dare they!" We can keep coming back to the breath, feeling its movement within, letting go of each thought as it arises and concentrating on the physical sensations that may be so intense as to feel painful. We might remind ourselves that each of us is doing our best given our current level of awareness. But the negative emotions go hand-in-hand with a strong physiological response – the body is in the grip of the emotion – and more negative thoughts will arise. It's hard to stay present; it's rather like an entity has taken hold and is trying to feed itself. A thought may pop into the mind of a similar thing that this person did previously, indignation and anger follow and the negative emotions are refuelled.

We're so good at holding on to our emotions that we've even developed a term for it in our language – 'emotional baggage' – but perhaps you can set the intention now to stop accumulating this poisonous stuff in your body. Allow yourself to fully open to whatever feelings are present in the moment; feel them as deeply as you can, and then set yourself free by letting go. Give the thoughts and feelings permission to move on as soon as they are ready, and stay present because the ego will strongly dislike being denied the opportunity to make itself *more* and someone else *less*. The word 'soften' carries with it the energy of 'letting go', and indeed sometimes my mantra as I process a difficult situation is, "Soften, flow and let it go." I will say this over and over to myself, and occasionally burst into song. Who doesn't love a short burst of the *Let It Go* song from the *Frozen* movie?! Well, my children, now that I pause to reflect on it, but I do keep my outbursts to the family home or vehicle rather than in public (and how glad they are about that).

As well as letting go in relation to our difficulties, we also have a strong tendency to cling to whatever it is that we have, with a deep fear of losing it. This includes positive thoughts and emotions. Yet all things in life are only temporary, so we doom ourselves to suffering by clinging to what we want and have, and pushing away what we don't want. Sometimes we even fear losing what we have so much that we push it away deliberately. A year or so ago, a participant of one of my mindfulness courses recounted how she watched her mind talk her out of having a good experience... she had woken up in a great mood, which was something that was quite unusual for her, and for a moment she really enjoyed the positive sensations of feeling full of energy, optimism and joy. Then her mind told her, "You know this won't last. You never feel happy for long, and this feeling is going to go. Misery will return you know, so you'd be better off just stopping this happy nonsense because you know that's not you – you're just not a happy person. Misery is safer – nobody can take that away from you." She had observed these thoughts as she neared the end of an 8-week course, and was startled to realise that she had rejected happiness, simply because the fear of losing it was so intense that she felt moved to reject it before it could 'reject' her.

Guides from Beyond

"The Guest House" poem by Rumi is possibly one of the most widely quoted texts in mindfulness trainings around the world, perhaps because it so beautifully asks us to shift our perception and awaken from the trance of suffering and separation. It draws our attention to the possibility of trusting that our present-moment difficulty has been 'sent as a guide from beyond' in order to teach us something, and therefore has great value:

This being human is a guest house
Every morning a new arrival.
A joy, a depression, a meanness,
some momentary awareness comes
as an unexpected visitor.
Welcome and entertain them all!
Even if they are a crowd of sorrows,
who violently sweep your house
empty of its furniture,
still treat each guest honorably.

He may be clearing you out for some new delight.
The dark thought, the shame, the malice,
meet them at the door laughing,
and invite them in.
Be grateful for whoever comes,
because each has been sent
as a guide from beyond.
Rumi

In addition to the seven attitudinal foundations of mindfulness that we've just looked at, we may wish to hold some other guiding words as further learning intentions through our visual-isation practices. These are not attitudes as such, they are perhaps simply natural qualities of awareness or maybe just words that carry with them the energy of the heart, but they tend to fade as we grow up: *playfulness, wonder, limitlessness, flow, connection* (with others, with nature), *cycles* (the breath, birth/death, moon/sun/seasons), *true essence* (the inner light that cannot be affected by our or other people's limiting beliefs about who we are), *delivering our gifts* and *tapping into intuition* (following the wisdom of the body). Perhaps it was a recognition that the process of growing up seems to shroud these innate qualities that gave birth to the story of *Peter Pan* in JM Barrie's mind. Like delicate garden plants, we need to tend to these qualities to keep them alive and help them to flourish; we can do this by nurturing them in daily life and also by intending to awaken them with meditation practice.

In order to lead your child in a visualisation that intends to grow some of these qualities, you simply set your intention, move into Weeble mode (dropping your attention into the lower part of your body) and allow the words to form in your heart and then be spoken once they arrive on your lips. It takes practice to be able to trust yourself to do this, so when you first deliver these kinds of practices you may wish to jot down some words to trigger your memory as you lead the practice, but please avoid any urge, if you can, to read the meditation from a script. You will most authentically deliver any practice when you're actually experiencing the practice yourself, and you simply can't do that when you're reading what is essentially just a story. Your mission, should you choose to accept it, is to connect with the child or children in front of you and deliver words that feel right in this moment rather than connecting with a piece of paper that contains a meditation script that felt right whenever you wrote it (or worse still, that contains someone else's words!).

I'll expand a little more on how I see some of these qualities as being relevant both to us and our children...

Playfulness

We can take ourselves and life so very seriously. This beautiful planet is our playground. Whilst treating it with care and love, it would serve us well to never see ourselves as being too old to play. Experiment with embracing opportunities for playfulness in your life and see how it feels. Dance more and let go of caring what anybody thinks of you or how your body wants to move. Jump in puddles, regardless of whether you have suitable footwear on. Giggle at every opportunity. Bounce on your bed. Make a den with the sofa cushions and have a picnic in it. Laugh, be silly, be childish. Sometimes this is the only way to see what is around us with fresh eyes. In the midst of a silly and/or playful moment, check-in with your body to see how it feels – do you feel more, or less, alive?

Wonder

Our fundamental birthright is a natural state of joy, and this is a state that's quite different from happiness. Happiness comes and goes, tends to be related to our life circumstances, and has an opposite – sadness. Joy has no opposite and comes from a sense of aliveness and childlike wonder at the unfathomable beauty of the Universe. We don't have to go looking for joy, and our life circumstances don't have to be favourable for us to experience it, we just have to uncover it because it's here with us all along. We can experience a joyful sense of aliveness even in the direst of situations, and when we move through life with a sense of *wonder* – switching off autopilot in order to do this – we naturally awaken the joy within.

Limitlessness

If we dream BIG and live with the attitude of gratitude, we tap into an abiding sense of Universal abundance. We have a choice to live in fear or in love; fear leads us to competitiveness and a 'not enough' mentality whereas its opposite – love – will always lead us to find abundance. Limitlessness is perhaps quite closely related to letting go; here we let go of self-made limits or the limiting beliefs of others that we've taken on, and we allow our light to shine. If we create our own reality, then we'd better get our beliefs in shape!

Flow

I see *flow* as being quite closely related to 'harmony', 'trust', and 'acceptance'. Given the percentage of the body that is made up of water (somewhere between 50 and 75%), it is no wonder that the word 'flow' has such a visceral effect on us. If you close your eyes and kindly say to yourself, "Soften, and flow" three times, then I could pretty much guarantee that you've just experienced a physical change in your body. When we entrust ourselves to the flow of life, we no longer fight against our direction of travel. We have a sense that perhaps there's a bigger picture that at present we're not able to see, but that everything is unfolding just as it should. We're aware that something hasn't gone 'wrong' when we experience difficulties, and begin to see each difficulty we experience as being the perfect teacher for this moment. When we're present and embodied, we may very well find that actually we are experiencing far fewer difficulties, and that our outer life circumstances have become much more favourable. When we stop fighting life and trying to control it, life stops fighting back. We allow ourselves to be carried and supported by the flowing waters of life.

Connection

So many of our difficulties in life stem from a sense of isolation that we begin to recognise as an illusion when we practise meditation. Quite opposed to a feeling of loneliness, what we find when we drop into the space within is a deep, abiding sense of stillness that is anything but solitary. We can intend for a meditation practice to foster a sense of connection, with others or with nature, by:

- using words that reflect a sense of common humanity, e.g. recognising that just like me, each of us wants to be happy, wants to be healthy, wants to be safe, wants to live with ease,
- promoting a sense of empowerment and connection by encouraging the child to choose the landscape of their visualisation themselves – perhaps they would like to imagine having friends or animals (real or imaginary) present in their practice, and
- suggesting that their surroundings offer them support, for example, "Noticing how the ground unconditionally supports the body." If you live in an area that suffers from earthquakes, this probably isn't a great line to use!

Cycles

An awareness of cycles brings us home to our true nature. All forms are cyclical, and arise and fade – there is an outward movement (expansion) and an inward movement (contraction) until the form returns to the formless. Formless, not empty.

Eckhart Tolle refers to the formless often as the "unmanifested", Pam Grout calls it the "Field of Infinite Potentiality" or "FP". If we are to be in alignment with life, we must necessarily become more in tune with the cycles that occur all around us so that we can come to know ourselves more fully. We can learn so much from the cycles of the moon (felt to be a representation of feminine energy and connected to water) and the cycles of the Earth around the sun (felt to be a representation of masculine energy and related to fire). Our menstrual cycles relate very closely to the phases of the moon; many women ovulate on or near the full moon and bleed on the dark moon (or sometimes vice versa), and the seasons of our year are obviously related to the cycles of the Earth around the sun – the expansion of spring and summer phases and the contraction of the autumn and winter phases. The cycle of the Earth rotating on its own axis creates our day, with the expansion of the morning and afternoon phases and the contraction of the evening and night. We tend to feel more yang (outward and *doing*, perhaps feeling more positive) in the morning and afternoon, and more yin (inward and *being*, perhaps feeling more negative) in the evening and night. Our own lifespan from birth to middle age represents the outward phase of blazing our trail, then the more inward phase follows where we move towards old age, becoming physically smaller and more inward-looking. Even our breath has the expanding phase of the in-breath and the contracting phase of the out-breath. Birth and death, all within the breath.

Delivering our Gifts

It is tremendously freeing for a child, and indeed an adult, to learn greater self-acceptance and recognise that *each of us* has unique gifts to deliver to this world. I remember feeling very fortunate during my high school years to be able to pass exams with only a moderate amount of effort. I also remember the struggle of several of my peers, and the frustrations of our teachers who despite their best efforts couldn't seem to have their explanation of simultaneous equations understood by these 'lesser' individuals in the class who they sometimes announced would, "Never amount to anything much." Modern-day education systems are coming to understand how misguided this old-school education system was, that placed some individuals as 'higher' on some relative scale than others. And yet the prevalence of the words 'stupid' and 'dumb' in our everyday language ('eejit' where I live!) means that on some level we do still value intellectual attainment above emotional intelligence and other forms of intelligence. Self-acceptance values *all* and recognises the value of our differences – we can really learn to be OK with where we are and who we are, and see our differences as complementary.

10

Taming the Amygdala

Tension is who you think you should be.
Relaxation is who you are.
Chinese proverb

If we're stressed-out, then there tends to be a level of activity in the mind that's very hard to work with – the mind is so full of thoughts that we might feel rather in a fog, and quite unable to think straight, let alone be able to observe our thoughts, emotions and physical state with any clarity. So the practices in this chapter are specifically aimed at activating the parasympathetic nervous system and soothing the pesky amygdala (there are actually two of them, so double the peskiness, but for ease of reference we'll go with one). I've included several exercises in this chapter for you to try out, and after each exercise I've added some notes with suggestions of how you might wish to modify the exercise when guiding a child. Choosing language that the child will engage with is the easiest way to help a child to stay present and enjoy the practice, although if your child doesn't enjoy the practice then please don't see that as 'failure'. It's a wonderful opportunity to explore attitude, perhaps drawing their attention to whether they can locate this sense of 'dislike' in the body.

When enquiring into the child's experience, for older children we can use language such as, "Ah, OK, you noticed that there was a sense of disliking what we were doing when we were paying attention to the breath in the chest area. I'm really curious to know if that disliking feeling was making itself known in the body?" We can pause for a response and then clarify if the child seems unsure, "Maybe you felt a heavy or tight feeling somewhere, or perhaps something completely different?" For younger children we might use language that's a little more creative, for example: "Ah, great noticing that you didn't like what we were doing! Can you point to anywhere in your body where you are feeling that 'not liking' feeling?" and if they can, then, "Wonderful! I'm really interested to hear if that feeling has a shape and maybe also a colour, and whether it's a rough or a smooth feeling, or something different for you?" Exploring experience in this way allows us to 'walk the talk' of the attitude of acceptance and reinforce that there's no wrong way to feel, as well as strengthen the mind-body connection. In addition to using the practices in this chapter, it may be useful to note that there's significant evidence to suggest that encouraging children to *name* their emotions results in a more relaxed amygdala. Perhaps our emotions feel less threatening when we're able to recognise them.

Because the practices in this chapter are designed to be soothing, they might work well for calming an anxious or restless child at bedtime.

Mindfulness of Touch

Touch is arguably the most interesting of all of our senses, and studies have shown how important affectionate touch is for our well-being. Affectionate physical touch has a strong physio-logical effect on the body; it soothes and calms, much like the warm embrace of a mother holding her infant. The good news is that we don't have to wait for someone else to give us a hug, or a pat on the back, we can actually do something similar for ourselves.

10.1 Exercise: Gentle Touch

You can do this exercise pretty much anywhere and at any time.

Decide to pay really close attention to sensations of touch in this practice, and intend to allow the sense of touch to hold you in the present moment as well as to soothe you.

Take a couple of deep, refreshing breaths, and then allow your breathing to return to its normal rhythm and pace.

Perhaps starting by bringing your attention to the sense of touch as it makes itself known to you in this moment. Are there parts of your body that are touching other parts? For example, the sides of the toes touching each other, or perhaps your hands are touching something right now? Are there parts of your body that are touching the floor, or a chair or bed right now? If so, how does that feel?

And now bringing one or both of your hands to the neck area and perhaps using two fingers to make relaxing circles against the muscles of the neck, wherever it feels good to do so. Go gently with yourself – your neck muscles may be quite tight, and we're just looking to warm and soothe rather than work deeply into the muscles.

Moving your fingers to just below your earlobes now, and making small circles along the jawbone towards the centre of the chin. How does that feel?

Not shutting anything out, as we experience the sense of touch. Thoughts, emotions and other physical sensations will still arise, even as we pay attention to the sensations of touch.

Using the fingertips now to gently caress the face, perhaps stroking the fingertips across the forehead for a little while, and across the cheeks. Maybe using the tip of the index finger or middle finger to trace slow circles around the eye sockets, perhaps pausing to make small circles at the temples. Intending to bring kindness and gentleness to this body as a small token of appreciation for every-

thing that it does for us, day-in, day-out. As well as everything else the body does for us to help us to stay in balance, it will take an average of around 650 million breaths for us during our lifetime, and it does it all without us having to ask.

If it would feel OK to do so, perhaps bringing one of your hands to the centre of your chest area now, and placing it gently against your chest. Are there sensations of warmth or coolness that you're now in touch with, as a result of placing your hand here? How does the pressure of the hand resting against the chest feel? Perhaps moving the hand a little, backwards and forwards or in circles, over the centre of the chest area, and tuning in to any sense of soothing as you do that. Is it possible to spend a moment appreciating this body for all that it does, maybe allowing the hand to deliver that message of appreciation through its kind touch?

You may wish to finish the practice by giving yourself a warm hug and thanking yourself for giving yourself the gift of touch.

Tip: you can deliver this practice to a child or teen pretty much as is, simply adjust your tone and suggest that eyes remain open so that the child can follow your lead if they're unsure what movement you're suggesting.

Relaxing Visualisation

The reason that visualisations are so powerful is that the body reacts to what's going on in the mind as if it's really what's happening – the body reacts to wherever the mind goes as if the body was really there. A great many people rely on holidays to relax them, but the effects of a holiday don't tend to last very long and unless the mind has found a new way to be in relationship with the cause of the stresses, people usually find themselves back in a stressed state all-too-quickly after their return. A relaxing visualisation is like literally taking ourselves on holiday, except that we don't physically have to travel anywhere and so it's a lot cheaper than the real thing, but with all of the benefits (except a suntan perhaps).

10.2 Exercise: The Waterfall*

Find somewhere comfortable to practise and invite the body to adopt a comfortable position, either sitting or lying down.

Setting the intention to bring an alert and kind awareness to each unfolding moment, as best you can, to get in touch with any natural inner qualities of playfulness and wonder, and to experience a sense of connectedness. Spend a moment asking yourself why this may be beneficial – perhaps having a sense that you may be aligning yourself more fully with life as you do this, and opening up to the fullest experience of what it means to be a human being, alive on this beautiful planet Earth.

Coming home to the breath now, by experiencing its soothing flow and all of the sensations that accompany that flow. The in-breath. The out-breath. The space in-between. Introducing counting if you find that helpful – breathing in to a count of 3 or 4 and breathing out to a count of the same number.

After a couple of minutes, letting go of any counting and noticing any sensations of contact and pressure where the body meets whatever it's resting against – the chair, the cushion, the bed, the floor. Opening up to the experience of the body as a whole and noticing what's going on for the body in this moment.

Resting for a few minutes in an open awareness of the sensations within the body and simply allowing the body to present sensations for you to notice. Each time you register a sensation that's uncomfortable, tense or painful, perhaps saying the word 'soften' to yourself and inviting the body to soften around this intense sensation, not so that the sensation goes away but so that you can be in a kinder relationship with what's here anyway.

Then becoming aware of the space around the body as it rests here, breathing. Space within, perhaps, as well as space without. And with each out-breath, perhaps letting go a little more into the support of the ground beneath, allowing it to unconditionally support the body as it rests, and allowing the body to do the same for the mind – unconditionally support it as it rests.

Slowly beginning now to imagine that you find yourself sitting or lying in a grassy glade, in the partial shade of an old oak tree. Either visualising or having a felt sense of being in this grassy glade. A gentle breeze blows and the afternoon sun is lowering in the sky. Rays of light in orange hues reach your skin, warming it. The air smells fresh and the breeze carries with it the gentle aroma of summer flowers from the nearby meadow. You can hear gentle rustling sounds as the breeze ripples through the leaves of the tree. You rest for a short while, strengthened by the light of the sun warming your skin; your cares and worries perhaps begin to feel a little more distant.

Beginning to notice the sound of falling water pulling your attention now, and as you turn your head to follow the sound, you realise that you're close to a small waterfall and at the foot of it is a beautiful pool of clear, sparkling water. Rest here for a while and listen to the sound of the water falling, inviting your body to soften a little more and inviting your mind to simply be.

Feeling the warmth of the sun on your skin and the gentle breeze caressing you. The grass beneath you feels soft, and smells like freshly-cut grass on a summer's day. The sounds of the water falling and different melodies of birdsong reaching your ears. There's a

117

strange but possibly comforting sense that this place actively welcomes you being here; it's been waiting for you to arrive.

Spend as long as you need to simply resting, or perhaps you'd prefer to take a dip in the pool at the foot of the waterfall, allowing the clear, refreshing waters to cleanse you and perhaps also to heal you.

Whenever you're ready, finding your way home to your breath in your body as it rests here, reading these words. Aware of the body being supported by whatever it's resting against and noticing what that support actually feels like right now.

Intending to bring any sense of relaxed awareness with you as you continue your day, and taking a moment to thank yourself for having taken some time to replenish your inner resources.

Tip: a teen may enjoy this practice pretty much as it is, but for a younger child you will need to adjust the language and leave much shorter periods of silence. Younger children may enjoy the introduction of some animals such as squirrels, hedgehogs, field mice etc., all of whom are very friendly (perhaps they can even talk) and will only come closer if the child wishes.

Soothing Words

Words, as well as images, have such a powerful effect on the body. A soothing words practice can harness this power, particularly if it's guided in such a way that you are invited to choose a word that feels meaningful to you – a word that is perfect for you in this moment.

10.3 Exercise: Soothing Words*

Find somewhere comfortable for your practice where you're unlikely to be disturbed, and sit or lie in a comfortable position.

Set the intention to allow yourself to relax and tune into a deep sense of peace, both in the mind and in the body.

Become aware of the sensations of the in-breath, and the sensations of the out-breath. Pay attention to any sensations in the nostrils as the breath enters and leaves, perhaps noticing the cooler air moving past the insides of the nostrils on the in-breath and the warmer air moving through the nostrils on the out-breath.

On the next out-breath, allowing any tension to melt away from your jaw, allowing your tongue to sit loosely in your mouth. Allowing any tension to melt away from the forehead too.

On the next out-breath, allowing any tension to melt away from the shoulders, and from the stomach area, and anywhere else that you notice any tightness or tension.

On each out-breath, letting go more fully into the support of whatever you're sitting or lying on, trusting in the support of the ground beneath.

Become aware of how your body feels as it rests here, and inviting your body to release whatever it no longer has any use for. Take a deep breath in, and as you exhale, say to yourself, "Letting go..." Another breath in, and again on the out-breath saying to yourself, "Letting go..." One last time, breathing in then on the out-breathing saying once more, "Letting go..."

And now resting here with nothing to do except *be*. Just being here in stillness, in peace. In fact, imagining now that you're actually breathing in the word 'peace'. Either visualising that or having a felt sense of breathing in the word 'peace' and allowing it to fill your mind and your body, and then imagining breathing the word 'peace' back out, or maybe breathing out a different word on *the out-breath. Breathing in the word 'peace' and breathing out 'peace' or a different word, for as long as you need to.*

Perhaps choosing to breathe in a different word now, such as 'calm', 'allow', 'flow', or simply 'love'. Choosing a word that feels right for you. Breathing that word in, allowing it to infuse each and every cell of your body, and then breathing out that word or a different one, again doing whatever feels right for you. Do this for as long as you need to.

Paying attention to how your body feels right now, and your mind. Remember what this feels like. Intend to keep any feeling of relaxation with you as you move through the remainder of your day.

Tip: adults and older teens tend to find this practice more difficult than children, because they're more caught up in conceptualising what it means to 'breathe in a word'. Children don't tend to have the same issue.

Progressive Muscle Relaxation

The purpose of progressive muscle relaxation is to 'reset' the relaxed state of our muscles. Often we carry so much anxiety and tension around with us as our habitual way of being that we've normalized this and become used to an increased level of tension in our muscles. The mind has come to see this as our normal 'default' level and so we often don't realise how much stress and tension we're carrying around in the body.

10.4 Exercise: Tensing and Softening

Find somewhere comfortable to practise in a sitting or lying down position where you're unlikely to be disturbed, and ensure that you are warm and cosy. Set aside around 10 or 15 minutes for the exercise, if you can. We will move our attention through the body, targeting specific muscle groups, with the intention of really feeling what tension feels like. You are the expert of your own body, so please avoid targeting any problem area and if you have a medical condition that hinders physical activity then you may wish to contact your healthcare provider before trying out this kind of exercise.

Beginning by setting the intention to invite the body to experience both what tension feels like and also what deep relaxation feels like and then let go, as best you can, of any need for a particular outcome.

Take several deep breaths and then allow your breathing to return to its normal rhythm and pace. Bringing an alert, kind and curious presence to your actions, and working systematically up or down the body, starting with one of the feet or at the head: tense quite strongly for about 5 seconds, so that you can really feel the tension in that area, and endeavour to target only one particular area rather than surrounding areas.

Then letting go of the contraction, inviting all tension to flow out of the area, as best you can (perhaps saying the word 'soften' to yourself), and rest in the relaxed state for around 15 seconds, observing any physical sensations.

Suggested muscle groups to focus on:

Foot – curling your toes downward

Lower leg and foot – you can tighten your calf muscle by drawing your toes upwards

Thigh muscles

(Then repeat for the other leg)

Hand – clenching your fist

Forearm and hand – bend your wrist backwards

Whole arm – make a fist and draw your forearm up 'Popeye'-

style

(Then repeat for the other arm)

Buttocks – tightening by pulling them together

Stomach – sucking it in

Chest – tightening by taking a deep breath and include the muscles in the back of the chest

Neck and shoulders

Mouth – open your mouth wide

Eyes – clenching your eyelids tightly shut

Forehead – furrowing your brows or raise your eyebrows

Tip: when guiding younger children in this practice it's helpful to keep the practice shorter and concentrate on areas such as feet, legs, hands, arms, tummy, shoulders, mouth, forehead and eyes. I would particularly avoid asking a group of older children or teens to tighten their buttocks unless you're happy for the practice to move into snorts and guffaws of hilarity which might take a very long time to rein in.

I hope that I've given you some food-for-thought and that you can see how many avenues are open to us when we're looking to create a relaxing experience. Some mindfulness teachers place less emphasis on relaxation as being part of a practice, keeping their voices quite day-to-day and the pace of the practice sometimes quite brisk. This is perhaps to avoid fostering the common misconception that mindfulness is a relaxation technique (it *can be* very relaxing, as a wonderful side effect, but it's also about so much more than that). However, many years of working in complementary therapies has taught me never to underestimate the value of relaxation and I haven't yet met a client who wasn't experiencing some stress in their life, so I'm all for relaxation and quite unapologetic about intending for the practices I lead to be relaxing.

Relaxation sounds like a beautiful tune flowing through your ears. It feels like being able to be all alone when you've had a stressful day.

It smells like the light scent of lavender drifting smoothly up your nose.

It's like seeing people look at you and not judging you but knowing they care about you.

It's like touching a lonely and sad child on the shoulder, reassuring them and having a huge weight off your shoulders because you know you've helped someone.

And it's like tasting sweet, soothing honey melt on your tongue.
Sophia, age 10 (who experienced some Connected Kids™ meditations)

11

Mindfulness in Daily Life

Drink your tea slowly and reverently, as if it is the axis on which the world earth revolves – slowly, evenly, without rushing toward the future; live the actual moment. Only this moment is life.
Thich Nhat Hanh

With very young children who are perhaps too young to practise more formal meditation, encouraging mindfulness in daily life will mean that they will grow up seeing mindfulness as a way of life. We can really guide them to hold on to their innate capability of bringing present-moment awareness to their everyday experiences and also to grow kindness like a delicate flower that needs nurturing, so that it remains first (not second) nature to them. A young child can be the most effective mindfulness teacher for us as parents if we watch how they use their senses (including putting everything in the mouth!) to explore their environment and how they bring such a childlike sense of wonder and curiosity to their every endeavour. They don't yet have an 'automatic pilot' switch, like us grown-ups.

Young children up to the age of around three are primarily in right-brain mode – mostly driven by their emotions and without the ability to balance their emotions with a sense of logical perspective. Strong urges of desire are not tempered by a logical perspective and an ability to balance our own needs and wants with those of others – "I WANT THAT BALLOON" screams a 3-year-old boy, not caring in the slightest that it belongs to a little girl who's unknown to him and who's wandering around the supermarket with her mother after having visited the zoo. Bringing logic to this situation will not be helpful – this is not the part of the child's mind that is currently engaged. Bending down to the child and empathizing with these strong feelings of desire and how it feels to have what we want denied to us, we can connect with this hurting little being and show that we understand how they might be feeling. We can help them to recognise that it's OK to experience a difficult emotion moving through us – there's nothing wrong – and that this is a perfect moment to bring awareness to the feeling of the difficult emotion in the body, to *be with* it, make space for it, and bring kindness to ourselves in this moment of difficulty. As we empathize with the emotions being felt, we make a connection with our child that is not possible when we stick to our 'logical/rational' left-brain mode of relating to what's going on.

Naming emotions can help children to develop an emotional vocabulary; learning to bring awareness to (and name) the wide range of different ways they might be feeling helps them to process and deal with what's arising within them, rather than to stuff their emotional baggage into a metaphorical suitcase to be carried around with them for decades to come. Many children I've worked with have been able only to articulate 'happy' or 'sad' as possible emotions to be feeling, even at age 9 or 10. Whilst our child is learning about emotions it may be helpful to suggest to them what they might be feeling, for example: "Sarah, I noticed that you were sitting alone in the playground just now and you had an expression on your face that made me wonder if you were feeling a little frustrated, or perhaps angry?"

The opportunities to practise mindfulness in daily life are limitless, and children up to roughly age 11 or 12 will often be very open to spending time with you engaging mindfully with activities. When making a smoothie together, we can bring our awareness to the colours, textures and weights of the different vegetables and fruit. We might bring them closer to the nose, one item at a time, to savour any aroma that we notice. We can feel the weight, texture and temperature of the knife as we lift it to cut into the fruit or vegetable. I'm sure you're starting to get the picture – we're just bringing an awareness that's kind, open-minded and intensely curious to our everyday activities, using all of our senses, and encouraging our child to do the same. As another example, when brushing our teeth, we can bring awareness to the weight, temperature, surface texture and colour of the toothbrush in the hand, and we can do the same with the toothpaste. We can notice how it feels to squeeze the toothpaste tube (or press the pump). We can feel the tap in our hand as we turn it to start the flow of water, noticing what the flow of the water looks like, sounds like, and even feels like if we choose to put a finger or hand in the path of the falling water.

Older children may prefer to participate in mindful activities on their own, once they know how. The following exercise is generally well loved by those of *all* ages. Here, we employ all of our senses to fully engage with the activity of eating a Malteser.

11.1 Exercise: Mindful Malteser-Eating

You can do this absolutely anywhere, but you might find it helpful to find a space where no one (e.g. other family members) will interrupt you.

You can guide your child in this exercise and you may enjoy promoting a sense of occasion by using a teaspoon to carefully and slowly lift a couple of Maltesers out of the packet and place them on a napkin or in a small bowl in front of your child, and then do the same for yourself.

Setting the intention to bring ALL of your attention to the mindful eating of a Malteser, and inviting your child to bring their curious attention to the Maltesers as if they're an alien from outer space and they've never seen a Malteser before. And even before you pick one up, really explore the outer surface of the Maltesers. Are they perfectly round, or are there lumps and bumps? Are they smooth, or slightly pitted? How does the light reflect off their surface, if at all? Are the two Maltesers exactly the same, or do they differ? Maybe you could use an index finger now to experience the sensation of touching a Malteser, and turning it over on the napkin or in the bowl, looking really closely at what is now revealed.

Perhaps lifting a Malteser up now between thumb and index finger, feeling the weight of the Malteser and maybe also tuning in, just like a radio, to the sensations in the hand and arm as various different muscles work in order to hold the Malteser and now bring it closer to your eyes so that you can really examine this little planet of a Malteser more closely. Bringing the Malteser close to the nose now, and noticing if there's any faint smell as the Malteser arrives close to the nostrils. Does anything start happening in the mouth or anywhere else in the body as the Malteser comes close to the mouth? Any saliva forming in the mouth, or anticipation in the mind about how the Malteser is going to taste?

Slowly touching the Malteser to the lips now, perhaps the top lip and then the bottom lip, and savouring the subtle sensations there… maybe it tickles a little as the Malteser lightly makes contact. Then opening the mouth, aware of the intention to open the mouth and then noticing any sensations in the muscles of the jaws as the mouth opens, and gently placing the Malteser on the tongue and allowing it to rest there. Is there any flavour now spreading across the tongue? What's happening in the mouth? Perhaps the warmth of the mouth is melting the chocolate on the outer surface of the Malteser – how does that feel? Staying with the sensations, as they present themselves, noticing any urge to swallow or to move the Malteser in the mouth. After 10 seconds or so, allowing the tongue to slowly move the Malteser and noticing any flood of flavour now; any additional saliva forming in the mouth, any urge to chew and to swallow. If you choose to swallow, noticing how that feels.

Staying with the experience of the Malteser slowly dissolving in the mouth and observing all of the facets of the experience as closely as you can, until the Malteser has completely disappeared from view. Noticing any lingering flavour in the mouth.

Tip: after the practice is the perfect time to explore the child's experience with them, asking them if there was anything new that they noticed about the Malteser and whether the flavour was any different than how they expected – if yes, then making the link between this exercise and daily life. In daily life, the mind tends to have developed the habit of tuning out into daydreams and also believing that it's more useful to be worrying about some future event or chewing over some past event than actually paying close attention to the present moment. So in the case of eating in our normal lives, the mind thinks it knows all about what the body is about to consume and so it tends to tune out. If the experience of being mindful with our Malteser-eating revealed something new or unexpected about the experience and showed us we didn't know everything about a Malteser, what else might we be missing in our lives by habitually rushing through them and not paying attention to the present moment?

Note that a strawberry, raisin or grape would be great substitutes in this exercise, or any other small item of food.

Here are some suggestions of daily activities that children may enjoy bringing mindfulness to, and you will no doubt see that all we're doing is inviting their attention to really inhabit what is already happening:

Children aged 1–5

- Getting into their nightie, or pyjamas (and it's a wonderful way to become more present in the wind-down period just before bedtime) – noticing different sensations as daytime clothes are removed, really looking closely at the nightwear, examining any picture or pattern, noticing any smell (perhaps of washing powder), whether they're soft or rough against the skin as they come into contact with the body – if there's a picture on the nightwear, is there a texture to this picture (perhaps it's raised), any sounds as the fabric moves over the body? Once the nightie or pyjamas are on, inviting the child to notice if they can feel the fabric touching parts of the body. Inviting them to notice how they feel as they prepare to go to bed – is there an emotion here? Perhaps there are several?

- Holding and cuddling their blanket or soft toy, noticing the weight of the object, how it feels to touch, stroking it against different parts of the body, e.g. back of the hand, temples, forehead, cheeks, lips. Noticing any smell, and whether it brings a nice feeling into the body to bring close attention to this blanket or soft toy.

- Feeling raindrops land on the skin, or the wind tickling the face and hands, or the warmth of the sun on the skin, drawing the attention first of all inwards and then outwards – noticing first the sensations in the body and then expanding the attention outwards to notice the sky, are there any clouds and are they moving fast or slow? What colour is the sky? As the wind whips up the leaves that are lying on the ground, is there a pattern being made? Noticing all the different colours, sounds, smells and textures of the world around. Feeling the contact between the feet and the ground as they notice the world around will help to keep them present rather than drifting off into daydreams.

Children aged 5–7

- Walking to or from school – noticing the sound of their shoes or boots tapping against the pavement, feeling the muscles of the legs work to lift, move and place their feet.

Feeling the air against the skin.

- Brushing their teeth or brushing their hair. Children of this age are still developing their fine motor skills and so need to bring quite a lot of concentration to the activity in order to make the movements required – this is a wonderful opportunity to direct the attention to all of the sensory information that's being received by the body in relation to touch (the weight and texture of the brush), movement (noticing the sensations in the muscles as they move), sights, sounds and (in the case of brushing the teeth) the smell of the toothpaste.

- Examining a toy closely. Play-Doh is always popular to examine, perhaps because it has a particular smell, a bright colour and a really interesting texture to poke and manipulate. Examining a favourite toy using all of the senses can be interesting in terms of the emotion(s) it can evoke, and once you've guided your child to really look, touch, and listen closely, you could finish the exercise by asking them to bring their attention to any emotion that they feel as they hold their toy.

Children aged 8–12

- Playing sport, such as football or netball, experimenting with bringing awareness to the position of the body in relation to the ball. Bringing attention to the muscles of the body working to place the body in relation to the ball and other team members. Bringing attention to the feeling of the breath moving through the body, the feet making contact with the ground, and clothing resting against the body.

- Making a drink or pouring a glass of water. Feeling the weight of the glass in the hand, noticing its temperature and texture. Turning the tap and listening to the water pour out, or reaching into the fridge to lift out a carton of juice, aware of the weight and colour of the carton and its temperature. Opening the carton, aware of sensations of contact and pressure between the hands and the carton, listening to the sound of the liquid pouring into the glass, noticing any colour, any aroma. Lifting the glass with awareness of muscles contracting and releasing to make this possible. Savouring the sensations of touch and any taste as the liquid enters the mouth and moves across the tongue.

Teens

An adolescent will generally need to have their logical mind satisfied prior to engaging mindfully with daily activities. They will want to know what's in it for them (the Malteser exercise certainly helps with that!), and leave an open invitation to share a mindful activity with them as-and-when they wish, for example eating a meal together mindfully.

Children of all ages (and grown-ups too)

- Baking – so easy to engage all of the senses when baking together!
- Making a smoothie and savouring the flavours together.
- Pets – noticing how being with an animal really helps us to be in the present moment because (a) animals are only ever living in the present moment – they don't worry about stuff; (b) the sense of touch is the strongest of all the senses to capture our attention and hold us present; and (c) the sense of connection with an animal opens our hearts and we experience unconditional love.
- Mindful movement – bringing us into sensing mode by directing the attention home into the body, feeling how this body moves and how it exists within space.

12

Let the Magic Live On

And above all, watch with glittering eyes the whole world around you because the greatest secrets are always hidden in the most unlikely places.
Those who don't believe in magic will never find it.
Roald Dahl

People sometimes ask what I do for a living, and the answer is very variable depending on my mood in that moment as it feels constricting to have to define myself in any particular way. Sometimes I am moved to say, "I help people to remember to keep the magic alive!" As children, somewhere along the line the magic dies. The weight of responsibilities and encouragement to become more 'sensible' seems to squeeze the magic out of us. I remember as a very young girl feeling that life was full of immense possibility. Unicorns, dragons, elves and pixies, fairies and fairy-dust, time travel. Then, somewhere along the way, life seemed to close down. There were laws, limits, boundaries, walls and ceilings.

Hundreds of years ago it would have indeed been magic to show someone a mobile phone through which one could communicate with another person thousands of miles away, or refrigerate food, read books on electronic devices, travel to the moon. The advancement of our society is led by those who see opportunities and possibilities where others see limitations. It is led by those who believe in magic! It's an open-hearted, innocent, childlike wonder kind of a magic, and children are wonderful at teaching us where to look for it. Chase rainbows with your child, make wishes, blow bubbles and send them up to the stars above, look for pots of gold, watch for fairies dancing in the long grass...

most of all, never, ever, let the magic end.

This world is so tragically full of suffering that sometimes it almost feels too much to bear for many of us. Magic inspires us to look for and create beauty, and to believe in the power of connecting to the human heart and the heart of the Universe, even when beauty is not what we see around us. Magic lifts us and moves us towards the seemingly impossible.

In our daily lives we can look for the magic, as Roald Dahl suggests, "in the most unlikely places." We can marvel at moments of synchronicity that occur when we put a thought 'out there' and watch the Universe respond. As I spoke to the head teacher of my youngest child's school this morning, she talked of how odd it was that I was there offering to teach the teachers at the school mindfulness as it was only a couple of days ago that she had been despairing over the latest cuts and wondering how the staff would cope with the stress of trying to deliver the same standard of education with depleted resources. She had looked to the skies above and asked for some help. The e-mail I had sent her, in which I offered to teach the staff mindfulness, had arrived that same day.

Many people look for magic in the form of white feathers, said to be a sign that angels are near and offering their love, support and guidance. Certainly it has been my experience that in some of the darkest moments of my life a white feather has inexplicably appeared, and I have been reminded in those times that however heavy my burden feels, I am not alone. Whether or not you believe in angels doesn't matter at all, but looking for magic opens us up to the possibility that appearances are not always what they seem and perhaps there are supportive forces at work that we will perhaps never fully understand or see, but may come to *feel*.

In our meditation practice, visualisation has a huge role to play in getting us in touch with a world of imagined possibilities, and in awakening us to actualise our full potential. Visualisation awakens that which is sleeping in us – our true essence becomes activated in each cell of the body and the beliefs which limit us start to fall away.

I hope that the following meditation demonstrates what I mean when I suggest that we use meditation to keep the magic alive, and also shows that creative visualisation is not just for children – there's something within visualisation for everyone.

12.1 Exercise: Fairy Door*

Find a comfortable and supportive position in which to place your body, intending to allow yourself to feel completely carefree, and approaching this practice (if you can) with a childlike sense of wonder. Set the intention to visualise or have a felt sense of the scenario that follows. Allow your eyes to softly close, if that feels OK.

Reminding yourself that there is no wrong experience to have during this practice and allowing your experience to unfold without needing it to be any different.

Settling your mind in the way that you're perhaps by now accustomed to – taking your attention to the sensations of the in-breath, the out-breath, and any pause in-between. Introducing counting if you find that helpful, and intending to allow the snow globe of your mind to settle.

And now letting go of any counting and placing the attention on the out-breath, observing how the releasing quality of the out-breath actually feels in the body. Maybe allowing the weight of your body to sink a little more fully into whatever you're sitting or lying on, letting go into the support of the ground a little more with each out-breath, and trusting in the support of the earth.

Inviting your attention to drop into your body more fully now, and resting with the sensations first of all of contact and pressure where the body meets the chair, cushion, bed or floor, then widening that awareness to include sensations within the whole of the body. Perhaps scanning down the body for a few moments, starting at the crown of the head and then moving your attention downwards through the body until you reach the soles of the feet (and don't forget to include your arms as you scan down).

Becoming aware of the space around the body as it rests here, perhaps even aware of the air touching the skin of the face, or the hands, and perhaps retaining a light awareness of the sensations of the breath flowing in and out of the body as you go through the remainder of the practice.

When you feel ready, and if feels OK to do so, bringing to mind your bedroom, either as it is now or as it was when you were a child, and taking a few moments to bring the details to mind. Recalling the sights, sounds, smells and textures of the room.

Imagining now that as you look around the room and notice details that perhaps you'd previously missed, you look down towards the floor and see a tiny little wooden door, only an inch or two high, that's quite close to a piece of furniture which is maybe why you didn't notice it before. As you bend down to examine the door more closely, you could swear that there's light shining through the miniscule keyhole of this fairy door and you can hear what sounds like gentle, melodic tinkles of laughter.

Filled with curiosity, you decide to touch the door, and immediately you are transported through it, finding yourself in a garden that's illuminated by row-upon-row of coloured fairy lights and hearing lively folk music playing somewhere nearby.

You can either enjoy some time in this beautiful garden just now, in which case you simply tune out of my words and allow yourself to delight in just being here, or perhaps you'd like to follow the sound of music? If it feels difficult to decide, then just notice any sensations in the body relating to that difficulty, reminding yourself that you can't 'get it wrong' – there's no wrong choice to be made here.

If you decide to follow the music, then first of all really feel where you are. You realise that your feet are bare, and you can feel the warm earth of a garden path beneath your feet. Noticing how that feels. Can you feel the gentle breeze touching your skin, or clothing resting against your body? What sounds are here?

The path that you've found yourself on seems to lead through a garden gate and out into a meadow, and you have a feeling that if you follow the path it will lead you to the source of the music. As you put one foot in front of another and follow the path, the tinkles of laughter grow louder and you take your attention to your feelings about what might await you. Do you feel curious, or excited, or perhaps a little apprehensive or unsure about what you might find? Just exploring your thoughts, emotions and sensations in the body in this moment.

You come to a clearing now with a small stream running through it and some tall trees surrounding, and realise that you have indeed arrived at a party, but perhaps not the kind you're used to. In front of you are hundreds of little lights, some dancing in the grasses and some hovering in the air above. You've arrived at a fairy party!

You find little lights hovering around your arms, and feel the fairies encouraging you to join them – they're so happy that you're here! Some of the fairy folk are making music, some are dancing, some are tending to the grasses, trees, flowers, animals. My goodness, some are playing party games and they're inviting you to play 'jump the rainbow'. As the sun shines down through the canopy of the tall trees, dappling your skin in golden, dancing light, it also passes through the mist of droplets above the stream and creates the most beautiful rainbow.

To join in the rainbow-jumping game, you simply need to use the power of your mind to move your body over the rainbow. Take 3 steps, then think 'up' and find yourself flying! You had expected to jump over the rainbow, but actually find yourself passing through it – an incredible experience of the most intense colours washing over your body and moving as if in slow motion; gorgeous ruby red colour, then bright orange, yellow like the sun, emerald green, sky blue, deep indigo, beautiful violet, then finding yourself on the other side of the rainbow.

Here on the ground, on the other side of the rainbow, as you pause to feel your feet in contact with the earth and the breath moving through your body, is a gift for you. It's exactly what you need right now. It might be a word, or phrase, in a card, or something in a gift box. What is it? Can you see? Perhaps you need to spend a little time with it before unwrapping it to find out what it is, or perhaps you already know.

Spend some time here with your gift, and enjoying the party for a while if you'd like to, or you could carry the gift back along the path to the garden, and spend some time there alone with it.

<a few minutes>

Then, in your own time, finding your way fully back into your body as it rests here in this moment. Bringing your attention to the sensations of contact where parts of the body are in contact with whatever the body is resting against. Take a moment to tune into how the body feels right now... what kinds of thoughts are here?

What kinds of feelings? What kinds of sensations? Bringing your attention to the sounds that are here in this moment, if any, and slowly open your eyes whenever you feel ready.

How did that practice feel? Was there any temptation to skip over it? Did your logical mind have trouble in seeing the value of the practice? As you tune in to the sensations that are here to be noticed in your body right now, are there any clues as to how you experienced the practice? For example, there may be sensations of tightening or closing-down which may alert you to judgements that you have made about the practice, or sensations of lightness in the chest area or elsewhere that may alert you to any positive feelings that the practice may have put you in touch with. Again, and I know I say this often, there's no wrong way to feel, but if you found the practice difficult or a waste of time, then the invitation is to bring curiosity to those thoughts or feelings. Perhaps you could listen to the recording of the practice to have a fuller sense of it.

Is it more joyful to move through life with a sense of limitations, boundaries and ceilings that constrain us, or with a sense of extraordinary possibilities? Which path leads to a happier, more creative life?

13

The Wisdom of the Body

There is more wisdom in your body than in your deepest philosophy.
Friedrich Nietzsche

My eleven years of practising Reiki have involved focusing healing attention on the body in order to bring balance, but for most of us the relationship with our body is a confused one. Many of us have been taught to believe that when there is an area of tension or pain we should try to ignore it as we shouldn't focus on the negative, and that's in a certain sense true in that it's helpful not to dwell on negative thoughts and feed them with our energies, but it's the *kind* of attention that's important. It's very helpful to give the body attention, but a particular kind of attention. That kind of attention is demonstrated in the 'Body Scan' meditation that we practised in Chapter 4 where, as always in our mindfulness practice, method and attitude go hand-in-hand. We endeavour to bring a beginner's mind to our experience and allow our experience to be our experience without needing it to be different from how it is and without judging it. We accept or *flow* with whatever *is*, welcoming into our experience as best we can whatever arises in our awareness.

When we focus on aspects of our internal environment that we feel need to be fixed, i.e. giving our bodies the *wrong* kind of attention, this causes us to feel worse – our minds focus on the gap between how we feel and how we want to feel, and try to bridge that gap by analysing the problem. Our bodily sensations, feelings and thoughts are intimately linked and as we focus on the gap then we may start to brood and start to notice unpleasant body sensations which then feed back into our feelings and thoughts, very often causing us to feel even worse about our situation, particularly when aches and pains start to creep in as a result of tensions in the body. In *thinking* mode, we want to fix what we judge to be broken. In *sensing* mode, we are content to 'sit with' not knowing, aware that a certain kind of wisdom – a particular kind of intelligence – comes from this different mode of mind.

Many embrace the Body Scan early on when learning mindfulness and then leave it behind once they're more familiar with seated meditations that centre around the breath or sound, but actually the Body Scan is a truly fundamental aspect of training ourselves to move from *thinking* mode to *sensing* mode, from *doing* mode to *being* mode. When my mother passed away in 2013, the Body Scan was the *only* practice that I felt able to do, albeit rather erratically, for the weeks following her death. Being with my body didn't feel as painful as being with my mind, and I remember being acutely aware of mouth ulcers, stomach pains and all sorts of physical symptoms that ironically helped me to feel quite positive in between the much darker moments. The enormity of these sudden physical symptoms reaffirmed for me just how strong the mind-body connection is, and I felt deeply that my ability to bring non-resistance to these symptoms would be the most helpful way to relate to what was happening. My journal entry on the day of my mother's passing in 2013 was as follows:

> *This morning I watched the woman who gave life to me lose her own life. She was sitting up in bed chatting to us as if we'd just popped over to her house for a cuppa, and yet the doctors told us her heart would stop soon. I told her that I loved her and that she'd taught us well, and then the monitors started screaming, along with a voice inside my head. I just feel like a little girl who's lost her mummy. There's so much darkness here.*

Days later, at my mother's funeral, my poem was read out by my beloved:

Those final words I said to you, "You taught us well, Mum."

You taught us that we should always choose in life whatever makes us happy.

You taught us not to worry about convention.

You taught us that there are no limits and that we should always fly free!

You taught us to be kind.

You showed us how strong we are.

You taught us that all things in life are connected, and that the spirit that infuses each of us is also to be found in the animals, the plants, the trees, the birds, the water. You loved nature so much!

And so when I'm sad, Mum, I'll look for you in the raindrops, in the wind rustling through the trees, in the hedgerow flowers, and there you'll be.

You taught us well.

One short week after Mum's passing and I was experiencing what many of us experience in the grip of grief – in the midst of such sorrow, life had thrust me firmly into the centre of the present moment – a curious and quite special place. My journal entry was as follows:

Indescribable pain has brought me to this place, to what feels like the eye of the storm, and there's so much beauty here. Thoughts rarely flit by. Colours are so vivid and vibrant, as if a bright summer sun is shining through after a heavy downpour. Sounds, smells and tastes wash through me, lifting my soul in gentle embrace before carefully setting me down again. I'm aware of the beating of my own heart, and if I pause to feel it, the beating of the heart of every person, animal, bird. I've never felt so alive!

My practices up until my mother's death had been very much

centred on awareness of the breath, with a light touch, and simply bringing my mind back to the present moment whenever I noticed it had wandered off. B. Alan Wallace calls the body, "an aggregation of mental and physical phenomena" and this phrase, for me, captures the essence of why the Body Scan meditation is so useful – our bodies are the containers for a whole host of ever-changing feelings, thoughts and physical sensations, and building a deeper connection with our body can serve to reveal so much that has lain dormant over the years as well as acting as an early-warning system to alert us to how we're feeling right now.

One afternoon I was driving home from a Mindfulness Studies training weekend at Samye Ling Monastery near Dumfries and I took a detour towards Livingston to collect my children before heading back to our home in Strathaven. I lived in Livingston until about thirteen years ago, and gave birth to my two eldest children in a hospital there. The closer I got to the hospital, the more noticeable the ache in my right leg became. My right calf is a place that I have often noticed, since starting my mindfulness practice, where I hold tension. I gave my right leg some more of my attention, feeling very curious about the sensations, and a memory flashed into my mind that I had long-since buried, of how the epidural had failed when I was in labour with my eldest son, leaving me in pain down my right leg that was almost unbearable for many hours. That memory appeared to open the floodgate for more memories to flood in – memories of the feelings of helplessness, despair, fear and all of their bed-partners. I recognised that my body was ready to release emotional toxins that had been locked down for 15 years, and so I allowed all of these house guests to enter and offered them the best welcome I could muster!

Mindful Movement

Along with body-based practices such as the Body Scan, we can really strengthen the mind-body connection through mindful movement – the more we strengthen this connection, the more the body will reveal to us. Movement turns up the volume on the physical sensations that are relayed to the brain – it becomes easier to remain present as there's masses of sensory information pertaining to the present moment to tap into. The body literally holds the mind more firmly in the here-and-now when we intend to focus on how it feels to move.

It's helpful to allow the gaze to fall softly to the floor just in front rather than looking directly ahead, as we can easily become distracted by judgements about our surroundings. As well as feeling into the muscles of the body working, a sense of contraction and release, we might be aware of the bones of the skeleton giving structure and strength to the body, we may be faintly aware of the pulse – the muscles of the heart pumping blood around the body in order for oxygen to reach every cell and for waste products to be removed, we might feel clothing resting against the body and creating interesting sensations in areas where our movement causes the sensations of contact between the body and the fabric to change as the fabric moves across the surface of the skin. We may be aware of swallowing. Eyes blinking. The movements of the body in relation to the process of breathing – often we rather forget to breathe fully, at least initially, when moving mindfully.

Walking is a particularly good example of automatic pilot at work; our bodies are in motion but we're usually completely in our heads as we walk along, busy analysing, worrying, planning or daydreaming. Let's learn how to bring our awareness to something that we do every day and bring our beginner's mind to the experience of walking.

13.1 Exercise: Mindful Walking*

Set your intention to experience walking with an awareness of your inner landscape – observing your thoughts, feelings and sensations as the body moves. You don't need a large area of space for this exercise, and there's no destination for the walk, we're just going to experience walking with awareness. Starting off in a standing position, perhaps with shoes off if that's possible, and becoming aware of sensations of contact and pressure where parts of the feet are in contact with the floor as the body stands here in stillness. As we feel what's going on in this body in this moment, we might become aware of lots of tiny little adjustments being made in order to keep the body upright and balanced.

Perhaps exploring for a moment how it feels to shift the weight in the feet, tipping forwards and backwards or swaying from side-to-side, noticing the changing sensations in the feet as you do that, and perhaps also noticing other parts of the body moving in space at the same time. Maybe you can feel the air touching the skin of your face and your hands?

If you find your mind wandering off at any point, then remind yourself that's just what minds do, and kindly escort your attention back to your inner world as it is in this moment.

As you decide to begin walking, first become aware of the intention to move, and choose which foot to lift first. Noticing the sensations of movement as the foot lifts, noticing various muscles tensing and relaxing in order to make it possible to lift the foot, and then placing the foot down. Aware of the sensation of the foot coming into contact with the ground and as you place more of your weight into that foot, perhaps noticing that it spreads out a little with that increasing weight, and more of the foot comes into contact with the ground. It might almost feel like your foot is massaging the ground. How does that ground feel beneath your foot?

Practise lifting, moving and placing with awareness of the physical sensations.

After a little while, expand your field of awareness to include any emotion or emotions that are here right now, and any thoughts.

Expanding your awareness to include what surrounds you, using all of your senses to inhabit this moment as fully as you can. What can you taste, what can you smell, what can you feel, what can you hear, and what can you see?

If you can, continue walking this way for around 10 minutes or so.

As you complete your walk, intend to transition into stillness and, with mindful awareness, come to a stationary standing, sitting or lying position. Feeling the body coming into stillness, and tuning into any sense of aliveness in the body that you can detect. Thank yourself for taking the time to, as Thich Nhat Hanh said, "Walk as if you are kissing the Earth with your feet."

Tip: always guide mindful movement (just like all practices) whilst engaging in the practice yourself with the child. Teens may enjoy this practice just as it is or you can introduce an element of walking hurriedly, as if rushing to their next class, then slowing right down again and experiencing how that feels, but when guiding mindful movement for younger children you may find that they engage more with a practice that uses nature metaphors. You could perhaps ask them to pretend that they're a tree, feeling their strong roots growing down deep into the ground, their strong trunk, and their arms are the branches. Guide them to reach their branches up to the sky, reaching up into the sunshine, and notice that there's a gentle breeze that's making their arms sway just a little. You might go on to ask them to feel the breeze growing stronger, making the branches of the tree move much more vigorously but also the trunk starts to move a little too. Noticing how this feels. Finishing with the wind returning to a very gentle breeze and then the air comes to a complete stillness, mirroring the body coming to complete stillness. Asking the child to notice how it feels for the body to come into stillness, and perhaps drawing their attention to the contact between the soles of their feet and the floor.

Note that you can play popular games such as 'Twister' as exercises in mindful movement, or indeed simply walking in the park – it's all about how you guide the activity.

13.2 Exercise: Body and Mind Letters

After doing a mindful movement practice with a genuine spirit of kindness and appreciation for this body and all that it does for us, write a letter in your journal or on a blank sheet of notepaper from your mind to your body (starting your letter, "Dear Body"), and then from your body to your mind (yes, you guessed it, starting your letter with, "Dear Mind").

What do you want to say to your body?

What do you want to say to your mind?

Don't think about what to write, just allow your hand to do the writing and invite your head to get out of the way so that your heart can do the talking.

And so the key aspect here in learning to listen to the wisdom of the body is the willingness to 'not know'; this needs to be balanced with the motivation to know. Westernised society is particularly uncomfortable with not having a fairly instant solution to any problem – a desire for a quick fix – but some situations can truly be dealt with much more wisely by resting in the state of not knowing… a 'sitting with'. There is always much for us to learn from whatever physical ailment troubles us, but chasing after the understanding will not bring us any closer to it. For example, frequent sore throats may alert us to some tendency to leave things unexpressed – things that need to be said. Always speaking our truth, lovingly, means that unexpressed feelings won't gather at the throat (and literally choke us!). Problems with our ears may relate to not 'getting the message', to not hearing the truth of situations. Eye problems may relate to not seeing clearly – perhaps only seeing through the haze of our filters and layers of misinterpretation. Shoulder problems may stem from difficulty, quite literally, in bearing the burden. Back problems may alert us to feeling unsupported in life. All these years of practising and teaching Reiki have affirmed for me that the body simply shows us what's going on for us and only asks that we intend to learn to listen to it. There is no blame here – I do not suggest that we are the knowing architects of our own health conditions – I simply affirm what science already tells us: the mind directly affects the body, which stores and reflects our imbalances.

Reflection

When some people refer to reflection they are referring to reflective thinking, which we might consider to be solely a cognitive activity – a 'deep thinking' about something. Reflection as I see it in the context of contemplative practice (meditation) is something a bit deeper than that. When, as part of our mindfulness practice, we learn to drop a question into the body – a process called 'reflection' – we are tapping into the universal guidance system by asking ourselves the question whilst in sensing mode. I'll call it the UGS – kind of like a personal satellite navigation system for life. Sounds pretty impressive, doesn't it?! And it is, but what a shame that most of us don't realise we have this built-in satnav. What a glorious opportunity to support our children in shaping their future by teaching them how to use it!

Our bodies cannot lie to us, and the energy that flows through the body is part of the Universe – quite inseparable.

We drop a question into the body, like dropping a silver coin into a well or like dropping a pebble into a clear pond, and listen for the body's response. Anything bubble up? Any images, feelings, sensations, thoughts arising? When someone says, "Meditate on it," what they're saying is, "Reflect on it." We can reflect in daily life, pausing to still ourselves and drop a question in, or we can make it a part of a more formal meditation practice.

For example, you've had a tummy upset for a few days. It started after felt your boss began behaving a little differently towards you at work, and you wondered whether there might be some redundancies coming up. You can choose to reflect on this situation by dropping in a question at the end of your practice, for example near the end of an SGRS practice (covered in Chapter 8). The question might be, "What do I need to know about my tummy upset?" Logical mind might try to kick in, and when a thought arises, thinking mode might get the train rolling with lots of analysing. You might start to have thoughts about what medication you should take and whether you should visit your doctor, what you might say to your doctor or to your boss, and what they might say to you. If you can, notice all of this and let the thoughts go. Try to just observe what arises whilst holding your metaphorical seat at the side of the train tracks, rather than hopping on that train. Intuitive mind might simply produce an image of a compassionate being, inviting you to feel seen and heard in your difficulties and not to feel alone.

As another example, perhaps your son and your partner are at loggerheads and you're not sure what to do, if anything. The question for reflection might be, "How can I help to heal this rift between my son and my partner – is there anything that I should do?" Logical mind might say, "Well, you should hold a family meeting and knock their heads together," but in sensing mode we engage our intuitive mind, which might say, "Be love. That's all."

14

A Balancing Act

Your hand opens and closes, opens and closes.
If it were always a fist or always stretched open, you would be
paralysed.
Your deepest presence is in every small contracting and
expanding,
the two as beautifully balanced and coordinated as birds' wings.
Rumi, *The Essential Rumi*

We can think of *thinking* and *sensing* modes as having different energies. We all, both males and females, are a mixture of yin (female) and yang (male) energies and it is interesting to note how much our Western society values the yang energy of thinking, action, outward-looking, doing. The yin energy is sensing, receiving, intuitive, inward-looking, flowing. Our life moves with the greatest harmony when we tap into the UGS (universal guidance system) using our yin or sensing energy and allow this to guide our action (our yang); in this way our energies are in balance and working in the way that serves us best. *Sensing* mode is the mode that powerfully drives us towards healing and is the mode that we tap into with mindfulness, and yet we currently neglect to heed its value, particularly in patriarchal societies such as ours. Neither yin nor yang is more important than the other – they are *equally* important, but by neglecting our yin qualities we have become very out-of-balance. The outside world is simply a reflection of what is within; the imbalances within ourselves are reflected in the world around us. Shakti Gawain writes beautifully about these different energies in her book, *Living in the Light*, and her powerful words point to the essence of healing – accepting, valuing and honouring each and *every* part of ourselves.

When I first read Dr Tina Payne Bryson and Dr Daniel Siegel's *The Whole-Brain Child* book, it was a revelation to understand through the lens of neuroscience (and in a completely different vocabulary) so much of what I already knew through practising Reiki and teaching meditation. It helped me to understand *why* our meditation practice makes such a difference to the brain and how we move through life. My understanding of male and female energies, through my Reiki training and years of observing my Reiki clients, tuning into their energy and learning of their imbalances, can be summarised as follows:

Left brain (controls right side of body) **Yang** – literal, conceptual, linear, associated with logic and reason, analysis, spatial awareness, language, literal.

Right brain (controls left side of body) **Yin** – emotional, experiential, non-linear, creativity, imagination, intuition, non-verbal.

It turns out that this ties in with what neuroscientists tell us. Bryson and Siegel explain that left brain is concerned with the letter of the law whilst right brain is concerned with the spirit of the law and that it's rather like the two hemispheres of our brain have completely different personalities. Where we often tend to 'go wrong' as parents is countering the illogical emotions of our child with a logical argument. This tends to result in a complete lack of connection. Later on I will explain in more detail the BE.LOVE method that I've developed for dealing with a difficult moment with a child; the general idea essentially being to bring presence to the situation, take a pause, and then take a moment to make a right-brain-to-right-brain connection with the child, soothing and allowing whatever emotions are there to be there, and when the connection has been made it is then possible to empower the child to make choices and bring a slightly more left-brained logical approach to the resolution of the 'problem', if one is required.

One of the most common issues that parents ask me about is how to establish a regular bedtime for their child that balances the need of the parent to have some time in the evening to themselves, gives the child adequate sleep time in order to feel refreshed for the following day, and doesn't involve the child running rings around the parent. With my own children over the years I have experienced times when it felt my child was a human yo-yo. Over a period of weeks there were what seemed like incessant trips out of bed each night with my little one proclaiming: "I need a drink of water", "I need a pee again", "I can't get comfortable", "Can you just rearrange my blanket so that it's tucked right around me", "Can you please open my door a bit more, it's too dark", "Can you please close my door a bit more, it's too light", "Can you stay with me a little bit?", "Why do I only get one bedtime story?", "I'm hungry", "Why is the moon out tonight?", "Why do elves exist in my book but I haven't seen any?", and countless other enquiries.

When my eldest was little, around 14 years ago, and I was still very left-brained in my approach to all problems, I would get very impatient and viewed what he was doing as a deliberate stalling strategy. Bedtimes became a battle, and it would sometimes take up to an hour before he would finally stay in bed and go to sleep. After a year or so of this, when telling a friend about the situation, she said, "He sounds a little insecure perhaps? Maybe you could just try reassuring him for a few minutes before you leave?" This seemed contrary to what was logical to me – he was looking for what seemed like an unreasonable amount of attention and I was trying to train him to need less of it. Nevertheless, I decided to give it a go. Each evening after his story I spent a few minutes silently soothing him. I knelt down next to his bed, placed my face close to his and stroked his hair. I would then quietly head towards the door and turn to blow kisses. He liked to blow kisses for up to a minute or so, which initially felt silly and almost moved back into a battle of how I *thought* things should go, i.e. we take turns to blow a kiss and then I leave the room. I blew kisses for as long as he wanted though, taking my cue from the slightly sleepy, contented look on his face, said, "I love you, darling, sleep well," and quietly left the room. To my astonishment, he didn't come out of bed! On subsequent evenings he would occasionally call to me (without getting out of bed) as I was attempting to turn and leave, and I would patiently blow kisses again until I realised he was satisfied; he felt cared for and loved. Over the coming weeks, the length of these kiss-blowing interactions decreased to a few kisses to-and-fro and then I was able to leave without any drama.

For a variety of reasons, which may include our natural inclination as sentient beings to instinctively move away from discomfort and because the Western world generally values left brain above right, a common strategy in children (and indeed adults too) is to suppress what's arising and retreat into left brain. For example, if your child doesn't get invited to a party, their body language can give us cues to their disappointment and sense of rejection, but they may say something like, "Well, I didn't even want to go anyway." In this instance we can again endeavour to make a right-brain-to-right-brain connection. When confronted with this situation we can turn our full attention to the child and really tune in to a heartfelt sense of how their rejection feels, softening our gaze and our body language and communicating our empathy. We might say something like, "Oh, sweetie, I know when that happened to me I kind of felt a bit sad, you know, a bit left out?" Then, watching the body language, listening to the tone of any reply as well as the words, we can feel into the best way to continue holding the space for the child in that moment with tenderness and compassion. Not a 'fixing' space, but a tender holding space, where the child feels cared for and nurtured.

Neuroscientists talk of horizontal (left brain/right brain) integration and also vertical (higher functioning and more primitive, lower functioning part of the brain) integration. Thousands of years before neuroscientists existed, Greek philosophy stated that we are made up of four elements – earth (the energy of below), air (the energy of above), water (right-brain, flowing, passive *being* energy) and fire (left-brain, active *doing* energy). Different words, but (I believe) same meaning. To be in balance, we must tend to the different aspects of ourselves, these different energies, and intend to grow those aspects of ourselves that are overshadowed by the opposite energy. For example, if we find that we lack assertiveness and are often saying "yes" to requests that leave us feeling overburdened and burnt-out, our energy is a little too *yin* and we can set the intention to grow our *yang*! Shakti Gawain in *Living in the Light* explains beautifully how our personality is made up of primary selves and how we can bring balance by nurturing our non-primary selves, e.g. independence vs vulnerability.

I met a man in Thailand earlier this year, an elderly gentleman who was very chatty, who knew nothing about mindfulness and thought it all sounded a bit newfangled and wishy-washy but who spent his days travelling the world giving motivational talks on how to keep energised and balanced. His secret? He did something new, every single day, that equally utilised *both* sides of his body. He had learned to juggle, learned to ride a unicycle, wrote and brushed his teeth just as well with his left hand as he did with his right, could write, paint and do jigsaw puzzles using either of his feet. It really struck me as I listened to this man that these are different angles on the same story – we are joyful and balanced when the brain is integrated and functioning more as a whole, and indeed when the heart and mind are integrated and functioning as a whole, rather than pulling in different directions.

15

Tips for Leading Meditations

Courage is not the absence of fear, but rather the judgment that something else is more important than fear.
Ambrose Redmoon

I hope in this chapter to impart some nuggets of wisdom in relation to the 'how' of guiding a child or children in a practice. If you have more than one child and they are more than two years apart in age (or tend to bicker or compete for your attention) you may find it works better to take the time to lead each child in their own practice. Also, leading a single child is a much less scary way to ease yourself into leading practices. On that note, I would humbly suggest that you avoid terrifying yourself too much and aim to start with a simple exercise such as 8.3 Heart Breathing or 11.1 Mindful Malteser-Eating. This will hopefully give you some confidence to try some of the other suggestions in the book if you haven't already, and before you know it you'll be ready to fly and lead a practice creatively without a book or script in sight. When that moment comes I shall be there with you in spirit, doing a funky-chicken dance to celebrate!

Before you begin leading a practice, it's helpful to give general guidance around what to do when you ask a question during the meditation, pointing out that it should be answered in their head and then they can share their experience afterwards. Note that some children may find it hard to keep their answers to themselves – they may be really eager to share their experience – and if you're only leading one child in a practice then this can be a really lovely interactive practice where you almost take turns in leading each other, but if you're leading more than one child then it's more important to reiterate the importance of answering any questions in the head so that the practice of others isn't disturbed. You may also wish to explain to the child why you'd like to lead them in the particular practice, but keep this very short and use any prior explanation as a 'hook' rather than as a lecture on mindfulness. For example, I recall asking my niece when she was four years old if she knew how to breathe through the soles of her feet. She looked at me with great suspicion and indignantly told me not to be so ridiculous. I replied, "No, seriously, it's really fun to do. Not many people know how to do it, but I'll show you how if you like." She nodded, and we began. She's seven years old now, and she still asks sometimes if we can practise breathing through the soles of our feet together. As a variation on the theme, she and my youngest son sometimes lie on the floor with the soles of their feet touching, and they imagine drawing the breath in through the sole of one foot and sending it out the sole of the other foot – in this way they feel like they're giving and receiving the breath to and from each other.

It's really worth spending at least 5 minutes before leading a practice, if you can, in a short meditation yourself. In impromptu situations like the one just described, that obviously isn't possible, but if you can (and particularly when starting out in leading practices) get in touch with the breath, follow its flow for a few moments, and then guide your attention into that grounded space of the body, still aware of the sensations of the breathing rhythm but with a wider focus of the whole of the body. You might want to place one or both of your hands over the centre of your chest as a soothing gesture, really intending to bring kindness to yourself and also topping up your inner resources. When you feel strongly rooted in the present moment, then find a space with your child where you're unlikely to be disturbed, and begin.

Always join the child in the practice that you're guiding, i.e. see it as a shared meditation rather than something you're imposing on the child or 'doing' to them. This makes the practice much more authentic – being led from sensing mode rather than thinking mode and from a place of experiencing the practice yourself – and also means that you're much more likely to get your pacing right.

Decide what you intend for the practice, e.g. physical relaxation, calming the mind, connection with nature (trees, animals etc.), safe space, sense of feeling supported, reducing sense of isolation, cultivating loving-kindness. Intention can be a mixture of things and/or can be very general – simply to be present in the moment with compassion. Whatever practice you lead, please be mindful of the attitude pointed to by the seven guiding lights (*beginner's mind, non-striving, non-judging, patience, trust, acceptance* and *letting be*) and consider whether your intention for the exercise includes nurturing any of the additional energies of the heart (*playfulness, wonder, limitlessness, flow, connection, cycles, true essence, delivering our gifts* and *tapping into intuition*) mentioned in Chapter 9.

To begin, adopt a meditative posture and keep your eyes open so that you can be in touch with how your child is doing. It's fine to soften your gaze by allowing your eyes to find a spot somewhere on the floor in front of you and move softly out of focus, rather than staring directly at the child. Softening your gaze will lessen the amount of visual stimuli reaching your brain, so allow you to find a little more stillness, whilst still giving you the ability to pick up any visual cues from your child about how they're experiencing the practice. When I started teaching my youngest child to meditate, when he was around three or four, he would often open his eyes in case he was missing something. Having my eyes open meant that I could be aware of this, and perhaps suggest that he close his eyes again if that felt OK, so that he could direct his attention to his inner world rather than the outer. When working with older children, particularly if they're used to meditation, I will encourage them to experiment with eyes open but with a soft gaze when we're doing breath awareness practices as this often has the effect of helping to make the bridge for mindfulness to enter more fully into our normal daily lives rather than just when we're doing more formal meditation practice.

When you're ready, intend to connect to the heart as you speak, and visualise things going well. Let go of any particular expectation that you may have for the practice. Connect to how it feels in the body when you feel in the flow; when you feel in alignment with life itself. Trust, trust, trust. Take a deep breath. Release. Become a Weeble, inviting the mind to inhabit the whole of the body and feeling that strong base. In particular, tune into any sensations in the area of the heart.

Use really invitational language with lots of options (you may have noticed that I use the words 'perhaps' and 'maybe' rather a lot!) and using lots of words that end in 'ing' so that the child doesn't simply feel ordered around. When someone invites us to do something, we're much more likely to do it, but when someone tells us to do something then a natural resistance can arise. We also want to empower our child to make choices for themselves and not to feel that mindfulness practice is just one more way for an adult to exert control in their lives. It's helpful to mix use of you/your, we/our, and 'the'. The word 'the', for example 'the body' or 'the thoughts in your mind', disentangles us from being so closely identified with this body or our thoughts as being who we are; 'we' and 'our' bring us closer to a sense of oneness and a shared human experience; 'you' and 'your' connect us with our own direct experience.

Try to leave plenty of space between your words for experience to unfold – take several full breaths before speaking again, and this will help you not to gallop along. Because you are experiencing the practice yourself, you will have a sense of words 'coming to you' or 'arriving' – I think of them as arriving from the heart. When they arrive, simply open your mouth and speak them, without judgement. Leap off that metaphorical cliff and trust that the ground will rise up to meet you. When it does, you will feel like a superhero, and indeed you are!

Guidance for different age groups:

0–3 Concentrate on bringing attention to the present moment through awareness of sensory information and developing the *attitude* of mindfulness with mindful activities and mindfulness of emotions and physical sensations.

4–7 Keep things light and short, use really engaging language and embody a sense of childlike curiosity. Short sound awareness meditations using singing bowls or tuning forks tend to go down really well, as do touch meditations (crystal, pine cone, seashells etc.) and mindful eating practices (e.g. strawberries, raisins, grapes). Mindful movement and then 8.3 Heart Breathing is a good combination to try if you want to extend the period of practice.

8–12 If children of this age are new to meditation, keep things short initially but soon they will be able to sit for longer. Children of this age will enjoy similar practices to the 4–7 age group but will be able to focus for a little longer. They will also tend to enjoy visualisations that make really full use of the senses.

13–adult Perhaps use visualisations a little less often – emphasis is more on being mindfully aware of thoughts, emotions and body sensations in this moment as a way of learning to be with our experience (whether good, bad or neutral) in a more open-hearted and even-minded way. That being said, if you have an anxious teen and/or one who is very hard on themselves, then visualisations may be very useful in promoting relaxation and also growing self-compassion. I've found that the teens I've worked with have been remarkably receptive to using guided imagery, with the following caveats:

- don't try to impose your taste in relaxing music on them – this doesn't generally go down very well,
- choose a scenario that an adult might enjoy – for example, a beach or waterfall. Younger children will enjoy a birthday party, a playpark, a ride in a space rocket or on a magic carpet, but teens will tend to find these very babyish,
- use age-appropriate tone and language – for example, if your voice is overly full of wonder and enthusiasm, your teen may start to giggle and lose concentration!

Guiding a visualisation

When leading a child in a visualisation, it's generally a good idea to initially guide a settling of the mind (this can be quite brief with children as they tend to find it easier to settle), help the child to ground their attention in the body to create stability, then use guided imagery in line with your intention for the practice. Visualisations, just like a story, have a beginning, a middle and an end. Adults require a practice to be quite logical, but children don't really care too much in my experience. For example, if you say, "Jump over the fence into the field and then close the gate behind you, finding yourself in a beautiful meadow full of wild flowers," adults will tend to move into resistance and get stuck for a while at the gate because of judgement that it makes no sense to shut the gate if you just jumped over the fence, whereas a child will be in the meadow and enjoying the flowers without a second thought, continuing to follow your guidance. So if you feel like you made a 'mistake' when guiding a practice then please let it go because (a) in all likelihood, the only one who noticed was you; and (b) you can't be fully present and guiding the practice from a place of presence if part of your mind is in the past, getting all critical and telling you that you're not very good at this.

Allow your intention for the practice to guide what

transpires, and then just see where the practice takes you. I honestly have no idea what journey we will go on when I lead a visualisation, I just trust some words to arrive – practices led this way tend to be quite magical and from the heart, rather than the head.

So, in summary:

- prepare yourself by taking a few mindful breaths and grounding yourself,
- set your intention for the practice (ensuring that this includes guiding the practice from the heart),
- place your body and invite the child to do the same,
- lead the practice with invitational language and use a tone of voice that is calm, confident, and relaxed while still ensuring your voice can be heard, and
- after the practice, ask the child if they'd like to share something about their experience (remember, all experiences are OK) or ask them to write or draw something about their experience.

16

Meditations for Younger Children

If every 8 year old in the world is taught meditation, we will eliminate violence from the world within one generation.
Dalai Lama

As always in these practices, please tweak the language to whatever suits your child's age and stage of development. The exercises given in this chapter are designed to be useful starting points from which to launch into your own creativity to bring any practice alive, so my suggestion is to avoid using the examples given below as scripts to read verbatim. Read the exercise yourself in a meditative way, i.e. having a sense of experiencing the practice as you read, paying close attention to your breath, giving your attention to the spaces between the words as well as the words, and then have a go at guiding your child in the exercise, trusting that whatever transpires will be absolutely perfect for what you and your child need in that moment.

You may find that the words that emerge are entirely different from those written here, and indeed the practice that you lead may morph into something completely different; if so then that's absolutely wonderful! My wish with this book is to convey the spirit of mindfulness and give a solid foundation of the 'why', the 'what' and the 'how', and with these example practices I simply hope to show that we just take the spirit of a practice and wrap it in language that is suitable for our audience. Our intention for the practice, which at the deepest level is always in line with the child's highest good, helps the words to form. For example, you may have a sense that your child is feeling a little isolated, a little wrapped up in their own world, and you might wish to hold an intention for the practice of helping your child to feel more connected. You might choose a visualisation that brings in a pet (either imaginary or real), as animals can be very potent symbols of unconditional acceptance and love.

To engage younger children, all that we actually need to do is:

- alter the duration of the practice to suit the current attention span (and don't be overly concerned about fidgetiness),
- adjust the language that we use to engage more playfully, and
- channel our inner child – wonder, beginner's (don't know) mind, curiosity, energy and enthusiasm.

16.1 Parent and Child Exercise: Eskimo Kisses

This is a wonderful exercise for bedtime, or in fact any time of the day!

First of all (and as with all of the exercises), ask your child if they would like to experience Eskimo kisses – it's unhelpful to force or coerce a child into something they're uncomfortable with.

Bring your full attention to you and your child. Bend down to their height or lift them up (if you can safely do so) so that your eyes are roughly at the same level. Use all of your senses to inhabit the moment as fully as you can, and invite your child to do the same. You may ask them what they notice about how their body feels in this moment – what are they aware of? Can they feel the touch of the fabric of their pyjamas or nightie against their skin? How does that feel? Can they feel movements in their body as the breath enters and leaves? Perhaps there's a sound associated with the breath? Perhaps they're even aware of the beating of their heart? Nothing wrong if they're not – just offering suggestions as to what they might be able to notice.

Gently and with full awareness bringing your noses towards each other and experiencing the sensations of touch and warmth or coolness as your noses meet. Savouring the moment of touch and then slowly and softly moving your face from side to side so that your noses rub together. Ask your child what they notice – are there sensations of temperature? Can they feel your breath on their face as you breathe out?

When first practising this exercise the child may not notice much, but they will learn quickly to tap into the detail of their own experience through the richness of what you share with them. After enquiring into their experience you can share any sensations that you're aware of, for example, "I'm feeling your warm breath softly tickling the area beneath my nose as you breathe out, and sometimes your breath reaches my lips. I can also feel your little hands in mine and there's a really happy feeling in my tummy and in my chest that feels quite light and fluffy like the clouds in the sky on a warm summer's day. Through holding your hands, I can feel little movements in your body and I'm also aware of little movements in my own as our bodies make lots of little adjustments to help us stay upright and balanced in each moment."

16.2 Exercise: Tracing the Flower

This exercise brings the attention to the breath and also to the sense of touch, so is great for helping the child to ground (bring their attention into the body) and is often very calming. It may be helpful to photocopy the image of the flower and invite the child to colour the flower in, then ask them to trace around the petals for as long as they like – going out to the tip of the petal on the in-breath and back down towards the centre of the flower on the out-breath.

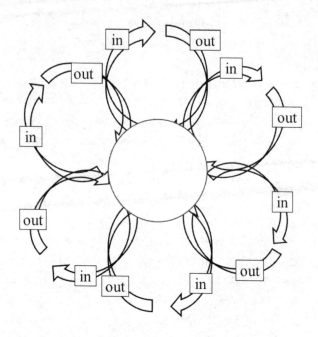

16.3 Exercise: Finding the Perfection

This is also a good exercise to use if working with a group and can be used with older children as well. First of all, find a small stone such as a tumble-stone, leaf or piece of fruit (or anything else handy that represents nature).

Invite the child to hold the object in one hand and notice its weight and temperature, then suggest that they gently touch the object with the index finger of the opposite hand, noticing the sensations of touch as they do that. How does it feel to touch the object, what sensations do they notice? Is it rough or smooth?

Noticing the texture and perhaps holding the object up to the light now. Does the light reflect on any part of the object, making its surface shiny? What is the surface of the object like?

Is the object perfectly symmetrical? If not, does that prevent it from being complete? Does that prevent it from being beautiful?

Would you rather that the object was different from how it is? Just noticing what answer comes up – no right or wrong.

Noticing any judgements that you have about the object and, as you breathe out, seeing if you can release those judgements and just allow the object to be exactly as it is. Being curious about whether it's OK for the object to be just as it is...

16.4 Exercise: Where's my Body?

Invite the child to run up and down on-the-spot very vigorously for a few seconds and then to pretend that their body is behaving like an out-of-control puppet – arms and legs waggling and wobbling all over the place (if this is OK for them physically to do). It's helpful if you can join in too, and if your child starts giggling as you waggle and wobble together then all-the-better! Alternate these activities for a minute or two, and then invite the child to lie down flat on the floor in a comfortable position. Flat on the back is fine, or face down, or on their side, whichever your child feels happier with. If you have a heavy blanket available, you may find it very helpful to drape this over your child – this technique is particularly useful for quite ungrounded children (often those with attentional-related difficulties or hyperactivity) who have trouble with proprioception (an awareness of their body within space). Using your own words of course, but leading the practice along the following lines:

Allow your eyes to close, if that's OK, so that you can explore what's going on inside of you. We can think of what we're doing as looking *inside* of ourselves instead of outside of ourselves, and to do that it's often helpful to close our eyes so that we can see in a different way. The way that we see inside of ourselves is to *feel*

what's going on.

Lying here on the floor, as this wiggly, waggly body comes to rest, how does this body feel right now? Just answering my questions inside your head, and then we can talk about what you noticed after our practice. Can you feel any tingling, or jingling? Buzzing or glowing? Hot bits or cold bits? Heaviness or lightness? Tuning in like a radio to anything that's here to be noticed in your body in this moment. If you don't notice anything in particular, then that's fine – there's absolutely no wrong way to do this exercise!

Can you feel any parts of your body touching the floor? What does that feel like, this thing we call touch? Maybe you can feel your hands resting against the floor or against another part of your body. What does that feel like?

I wonder if you can put your hands on your tummy now, and see if your hands move as you breathe in. Does your tummy get a little bigger as you breathe in? Do your hands fall a little as you breathe out and your body lets go of the breath? Keep breathing with your hands on your tummy for a few breaths and keep noticing what happens and how it feels.

And now I'm going to ask you to place your hands down by your sides, perhaps a little way away from the sides of your body, and to hop your attention around your body. I'll name a body part, and then you see if you can hop your attention there – see if you can find the body part and see how it feels, but without looking at it, and without moving it. If you don't feel like paying attention to a particular body part, then just skip it, no problem at all.

Hopping your attention into your feet now. Can you feel anything there? If you don't notice anything, that's fine.

Can you hop your attention into your ankles now? Anything there?

Now travelling your attention from your ankles through your legs until you find your knees. Can you find your knees without looking at them and without moving them?

Now letting go of your knees and hopping your attention into your thighs, so the top part of your leg between your knees and your bottom. Can you find your thighs? Perhaps you can feel the backs of your thighs touching the floor? If so, how does that feel?

Now hopping your attention into your bottom and seeing if you can feel parts of it resting against the floor? (Sometimes there's some giggling here, but that's OK.)

Now bring your attention into your belly. What's going on in your belly right now? Any gurgles or bubbles? Any grumbly, hungry feelings? Any full feelings or heavy feelings?

And now hopping your attention in your chest and seeing if you can feel what's going on there. Perhaps you can feel your chest moving a little as you breathe in, and as you breathe out?

Seeing if you can hop your attention into your back now – the whole of your back – noticing if there are some sensations of contact where your back is touching what you're lying on? If there are, what does that feel like?

Seeing if you can find your arms now with your attention, the shoulders, the tops of the arms, the elbows, the lower parts of the arms, the hands, fingers and thumbs. Hopping your attention into the whole of your arms and seeing if there's anything here to be noticed.

And, finally, hopping your attention into your neck and throat, your head and your face, including your mouth and lips, your nose, your cheeks, your eyes, your eyebrows and your forehead, the top of your head, the sides of your head, including your ears, and the back of your head. As you pay attention to how it feels in your neck and your head, can you feel any sensations of touch where your head is resting against something? Can you feel the air touching the skin of your face? No wrong answer, just being curious.

Finishing now by putting your attention into the WHOLE of your body now, as it lies here. Perhaps for a few breaths imagining that you're breathing in through the bottoms of your feet, up into your chest, and then breathing out through the top of your head. So breathing in through your feet, and breathing out for your head, just for a few breaths. It might seem like a very odd thing to imagine, but just see if you can give it a try. If it feels too difficult, then just spend a few moments resting here, giving your mind and your body a lovely rest.

Tip: younger children will often not know their right from their left, so guide this practice by saying "knees" rather than "left knee" or "right knee" but you can give guidance that if it feels difficult to pay attention to both knees then they can just explore one at a time.

Further ideas for younger children

Here are some further ideas for practices with younger children. I hope they help you to get creative:

Singing bowls – so far, amongst the hundreds of children I've worked with, I've found only two who weren't particularly enamoured with the singing bowl. That's a pretty good hit-rate! I've used it in so many different ways – in sound awareness practices where the child follows the sound and perhaps imagines breathing in the sound, but also as a mindful activity (children from around the age of 8 will be able to make the bowl sing by moving the beater around the outside edge of the bowl keeping the contact consistent until, very beautifully, the bowl begins to sing).

Mandala colouring – mandalas are essentially sacred circles and you may be surprised to realise that mandalas can be found everywhere if we pay attention. Mandala is a Sanskrit word that, roughly translated, means 'circle' or 'centre'. A shape with no beginning and no end, representing the endless cycle of life. There's a link in Appendix B to a free resource for downloadable mandalas for printing, and you can encourage your child to choose one that feels right for them and to spend some time mindfully colouring in, either with their dominant or non-dominant hand. Colouring in with the non-dominant hand better integrates the hemispheres of the brain, studies suggest.

Circle of kindness – you and your child sit with your right hand facing palm-down and left hand facing palm-down, and your right hand hovering above their left hand and your left hand hovering beneath their right hand. Each of you imagines breathing in kind wishes through the palm of the left hand and breathing out kind wishes through the palm of the right hand. Perhaps finishing the practice by seeing how it feels to send kind wishes out of the right hand and receive kind wishes through the palm of the left. Does it feel different? This exercise can easily be adapted to a group of children, sitting in a circle, perhaps in a nursery or primary school setting.

Quotes from primary school children (aged 9 and 10) who experienced a 6-week course with me:

"I used it (meditation) when I was on the couch with my dog and I was so angry with my sister. I closed my eyes and thought about my favourite place to be. I also used it in my bed because I could not sleep."

"I really enjoyed meditation because we get to take our shoes off and relax in school. It has really helped me to sleep at night."

"I enjoyed doing meditation with you. All of the stuff we have done is so so cool and so are you! I could never forget doing meditation with you and every night I do it. Sometimes I can't get to sleep at night and before I used to watch TV but now I can go to sleep. Sometimes I do meditation with my gerbil and it's so fun!"

"My favourite time was when you brought the singing bowls because it has a nice sound."

"I enjoyed meditation and I loved smelling the colour therapy bottles and getting to hit the bowls. My favourite part was getting to go to a place where I've never imagined."

"I enjoyed meditation because it helped me relax more. I used meditation one day when I couldn't get to sleep. My favourite part was being able to lie down at school."

"It was good when we went to our happy place because I liked it when it was all quiet and calm. I learned how to keep more control of myself."

"Thank you for all the meditation and showing us all the cool things like Tibetan singing bowls... I learned how to feel happy when I got sad and I've used meditation to make me feel happy at home."

17

Meditations for Teens

"Worst Day Ever?"
Today was the absolute worst day ever
And don't try to convince me that
There's something good in every day
Because, when you take a closer look,
This world is a pretty evil place.
Even if
Some goodness does shine through once in a while
Satisfaction and happiness don't last.
And it's not true that
It's all in the mind and heart
Because
True happiness can be attained
Only if one's surroundings are good
It's not true that good exists
I'm sure you can agree that
The reality
Creates
My attitude
It's all beyond my control
And you'll never in a million years hear me say
Today was a very good day
Now read it from bottom to top, the other way,
And see what I really feel about my day.
— Chanie Gorkin (aged 16)

Teens are moving through a phase of life where they seek to find their place in the world and strengthen their identity as individuals. As we grow up, much of our identity is tied to that of our parents, and so it is perhaps natural then that teens often feel the need to strike out on their own and rebel against their parents, because rejecting who they know they are not may in some way propel them towards who they are. Anything that a parent is interested in is commonly immediately rejected by a teen, and so tread cautiously with your enthusiasm about mindfulness (if, indeed, you feel enthusiastic about it!). We might be absolutely certain that mindfulness could make a world of difference to the difficulties that our teen is experiencing, but we can only gently sow a seed of possibility and hope that one day it will germinate.

Perhaps offer to buy an album of pre-recorded meditations for your teen, and see how the offer is received – it often isn't 'cool' to practise alongside a parent and the tiny seed of interest may indeed take roots and flourish if it isn't smothered with too much attention by a well-meaning parent. There are some suggestions of appropriate recordings in Appendix B – Resources for Children. Adolescents are often quite receptive to the same kinds of practices that adults find helpful, and so you can also perhaps offer them the meditation recordings that accompany this book at www.heathergrace.co.uk/AwakeningChildPractices.

Adult participants of mindfulness courses often cite the 'Three Minute Breathing Space' and the 'Self-Compassion Break' as the most useful practices that they learned on the course, and I have found them to be very well received by teens (with a tiny bit of tweaking). I prefer to call the practices MOP (Moment of Presence) and MOK (Moment of Kindness) respectively. They are, of course, longer in duration than a single moment, but they are very short, practical and portable exercises that, when practised regularly, can completely transform the quality of our lives.

17.1 Exercise: MOP (Moment of Presence)

This exercise has a shape like an hourglass – it has a broad focus for one minute or so at the beginning, a narrow focus in the middle for another minute or so, and then a broad focus at the end for the last minute.

Bringing your attention to what's going on for you right now, in this very moment. Maybe you could ask yourself how you're feeling, speaking to yourself in your mind's eye in a really gentle and kind way – a way that shows that you really care.

Noticing what's going on in the body – any particular physical sensations to be noticed?

Noticing any emotion or emotions that are here. Perhaps there's something here that you can't quite put your finger on, in which case rather than analysing what it could be, simply notice that an unnameable feeling is here.

What kinds of thoughts are here? Worried thoughts? Daydreaming thoughts? Planning thoughts? Judgmental thoughts? Random thoughts? No wrong answer, just noticing.

Then for a minute or so, zooming in our attention to focus just on the breath for between 6 and 10 breaths – you choose how many. Finding the place in your body where you're most aware of the feeling of the breath moving in and out. Focusing on the how it feels in the body to breathe in, and how it feels as the body releases the breath.

And now zooming out again to have a sense of the bigger picture. Aware of the body resting here, points of contact between the body and whatever it's resting against. Widening the field of our awareness to include everything – feelings, thoughts, physical sensations, sounds, smells, tastes, textures, and lastly sights (opening your eyes slowly if they've been closed).

Is it possible to see the thoughts, emotions and physical sensations simply as experiences moving through you in this moment, rather than who you actually are?

Finishing the practice with an intention to bring a quality of alert, curious awareness into the remainder of the day.

17.2 Exercise: MOK (Moment of Kindness)

This is a practice to engage with whenever you notice a moment of difficulty – for example, a difficult thought, a difficult emotion, a difficult physical sensation, or a difficult situation. There are three steps to the practice:

1. Notice that there's a moment of difficulty here and take a moment to pause, place one or both of your hands in the centre of your chest with the intention of soothing yourself. Feel your feet on the floor and resolve to be present for yourself in this time of difficulty. See if you can give yourself permission to really feel whatever it is that you're feeling, reminding yourself that there's no wrong way to feel. Feeling any sensations in the chest area that result from one or both of your hands being placed there – perhaps there are sensations of warmth, or coolness, and gentle pressure.

2. Difficulties are part of everyone's life – part of this 'messy' experience of being human. Around the world in this moment there will be many thousands of people who feel exactly the same way, or very similarly. You are not alone.

3. Intend to bring kindness to yourself in this moment, not as a way to make yourself feel better or to make the feelings go away, but because it hurts to experience a difficulty and everyone deserves to be tended to in times of difficulty. You deserve kindness. What does kindness look like in this moment?

So, in summary:

1. Notice there's a moment of difficulty and place a hand (or hands) on chest.
2. Remind yourself that difficulties are part of everyone's life and you are not alone.
3. Intend to show yourself kindness. Say to yourself, "May I be kind to myself in this moment" or words to that effect; use your own words and choose words that feel soothing and kind.

You can invite your teen to practise along with you if they would like to, perhaps listening to a recorded meditation together or taking a few minutes to do a MOP practice together. Make it an open invitation and make it clear that they can get up and leave anytime.

The following practice is a teen version of the Body Scan meditation. It's a longer practice that teens are most likely to find useful at bedtime in order to unwind a little. You could record it for them on their mobile phone (there are plenty of free voice-recording apps) or alternatively the practice is available as a recording on my *Wild and Precious Life* album for teens – details in Appendix B.

17.3 Exercise: Bodykind

Lying down for this meditation, if you can. Ensure that you're warm and comfortable, perhaps lying with a blanket over you. In this practice we're just going to take our kind attention slowly around the body and see how each part is feeling. Our bodies do so many things for us in each moment of every day, and we don't tend to take time to notice very much what's going on with them. We often don't even like them very much, and spend much of our time wishing that they were different! But we would live in a very boring world if all bodies were the same...

Just lying here, breathing, and having a sense of the whole of the body just resting here. Aware of the whole of the body from the top of the head down to the tips of the toes, from the back of the body right through to the front, and from one side right across to the other side. As you breathe out, inviting your body to soften and sink more deeply into whatever you're lying on.

Imagining now that there's a blanket resting over the body that is a blanket of kindness. Notice if that blanket, in your mind's eye, has a particular colour. You might 'visualise' this blanket, including its texture and colour, or simply have a felt sense that it's here. What is the colour of kindness for you? How does that blanket feel against your body? Maybe for you it feels like a blanket of a white or coloured light rather than a fabric.

With the blanket of kindness reminding us to go gently and kindly with ourselves, taking your kind attention into the very top of your head now and tuning in to any physical sensations that are there to be noticed. Perhaps there's a warmth, or a coolness, a tingle or a glow. Maybe there's an itch, a twinge or a prickle. Or maybe there's no sensation there at all to be noticed right now, and that's fine, just registering a blank when you don't find any sensations at any point during the practice. Expanding your field of curious awareness now to include your forehead, eyebrows, eyes and eyelids, nose, cheeks, lips, tongue, teeth, jaw, the sides of your head including your ears, the back of the head. Even tuning into your brain. How does the whole of your head feel in this moment? What physical sensations can you feel?

Imagining now that you're breathing in through a little hole in the top of your head down into your lungs, and then breathing back out through the tiny hole in the top of your head. Being playful with this – it might feel weird at first but see if you can give it a go.

On the next out-breath, letting go of the head and neck and swallowing down to carry your attention into the throat and neck, noticing how those areas feel. What sensations are here to be noticed?

Perhaps there's a warmth, a tingling or a glowing sensation here, or a coolness, or something else? Breathing into, and out from, your neck and throat now, and noticing how that feels.

On the next out-breath letting go of the throat and neck and allowing them to dissolve in your mind's eye, and feeling into your shoulders now. How do your shoulders feel right now, in this moment? They might feel completely different in the next moment, but how do they feel in this moment? And on the next out-breath, letting go of your awareness of your shoulders and allowing your attention to slip down into the chest area. So taking in your ribcage and the whole of your chest area, front and back.

What feelings do you notice as you breathe in and out? Are you aware of any muscles working? And on the next out-breath, allowing your kind attention to move down your body a little bit, into your stomach area, and bringing a kind attention to your stomach, how does your stomach feel, right now? And taking the attention round to the back of the stomach area now, so your back at the height of your stomach area. How does that feel?

As you breathe in and out, perhaps you're aware of sensations of contact between your back and the floor or the bed as you lie here. Expanding your attention now to include the whole of your back. How does your back feel in this moment?

On the next out-breath, letting go of the awareness of your back and letting your kind attention slip slowly into the abdomen, so that area of your body that's roughly level with your belly-button. That whole section of your body that includes your bottom, and your hips. How does that area feel right now?

On the next out-breath, letting go of these areas and allowing your attention to gently slip down to your thighs, noticing how these areas feel, from just above your knees to your hip bones. What physical sensations are there to be noticed?

On the next out-breath, letting go of this area of the body and taking your kind attention gently down into the knees. How do your knees feel right now?

Any time you notice thoughts, just letting them go, as if you're watching clouds in a sunny sky. Not needing to hold on to the clouds, just letting them drift away. And then bringing your attention back to your knees. And on the next out-breath, letting go of your awareness of your knees and taking your attention down into your lower legs from just above your ankles to just below your knees, so the area of your shins and your calf muscles. What do you feel in those areas? Can you feel any warmth, or coolness or tingling? Any sensations of contact where the lower legs are touching whatever you're lying on?

Perhaps you can't feel anything in this area, and so just registering a blank. We're not looking to change our experience, we're just noticing our experience as best we can, in all of the detail that we can. And quite often when we start doing this practice, we don't *notice much. And each time we do it, we notice more and more. On the next out-breath, letting go of the awareness of the lower legs and taking the attention into the ankles and the sides of the feet, and the tops of the feet, and the bottoms of the feet – the soles – what can you feel in your feet?*

Perhaps with a little bit of practice, you can start to notice differences in sensations between your toes! And so you can take your full attention into your big toes, and then you can deliberately choose to 'hop' your attention along into the next toe, and then the next, until you reach the little toes. How does that feel?

Each time you do this practice, you might surprise yourself by feeling a little more than the last time. You are learning to move your energy around your body.

And on the next out-breath, releasing the attention from the toes and just noticing the breath. Lying here, breathing, with this blanket of kindness resting over the body. Perhaps congratulating yourself for taking some time for you, and for taking the time to come home to your body. Maybe there's a sense that you've just done something pretty special for yourself.

Additional exercises for teens

In addition to many of the adult practices scattered through the book, teens may also enjoy:

- Mindful check-ins – asking them in this moment, what's your weather pattern? (Answers can vary from 'stormy' to 'sunny with clear, blue skies', and from 'hailstones forecast' to 'cloudy with a chance of meatballs'.)
- Mindfulness bells via an app that causes their mobile phone to vibrate at random intervals as a reminder to become present.

- Sticky dots as a low-key but potentially very effective way of helping them to remember to be mindful. You could even have a colour system, for example: red dot means to take your attention into grounding, noticing the feet on the floor, bottom in a chair; blue dot means to pay attention to your feelings; yellow dot means to bring to mind something you feel you've done to the best of your ability today; green dot means to send kind wishes to someone; pink dot means to take a moment to find 3 small things to be grateful for. I've included a link to the kind of sticky dots I'm referring to in Appendix B – Resources for Children. The colours of the dots link the energy centres that are being developed with an activity that develops that energy centre. If you're interested in learning more about colour for bringing balance, then June McLeod's book *Colours of the Soul* is a great resource for further learning.
- A Mindfulness meditation app such as Mindfulness Training App, Mindfulness Daily, Insight Timer, Headspace or similar.

Not interested?

If you do meet resistance when encouraging your teen to explore mindfulness, this is the perfect opportunity to remind yourself of the seven guiding lights:

- beginner's mind – be open to not knowing how things will turn out and keep an open mind, always viewing each moment with fresh eyes,
- non-striving – no need to get anywhere else in this moment than exactly where you are,
- non-judging – let go of judging your teen, they are acting from their current level of awareness which is different from yours,

- patience – allow the duckling to make its way out of its shell in its own time,
- trust – trust yourself, and trust life itself; we cannot know what the future holds but we can trust in the journey,
- acceptance – allow yourself to feel whatever it is that you feel, and allow your teen to do the same,
- letting go – let go of the need to control everything, let go of your fears about how your teen will turn out; trust them, love them, accept them, and they will surprise you.

18

At the Heart of it All – BE.LOVE

What counts is not just that we believe we love them uncondi-
tionally, but that they feel loved in that way.
Alfie Kohn

When we communicate with friends, acquaintances, teachers and even strangers, we tend to present the version of ourselves that is our 'public' face – the presentable side of ourselves that is censored. In family relationships we let our guard down and our family members get the real, uncensored, warts 'n' all version of us. This is why family situations tend to be so full of conflict, and are therefore the most perfect vehicle for healing and transformation. Our family relationships reflect to us most clearly the work that needs to be done. Without this reflection we would be blissfully unaware of many of our expectations, assumptions, patterned behaviours and intolerance. Family brings our shadows out to play, and family life is often anything but peaceful and harmonious.

Our role in interacting with anyone, including children, is best served when we drop the 'I know best' attitude and demonstrate that we don't always need to be right and that we are OK with not knowing – that we're willing to *be with* a situation without immediately understanding it fully and knowing what to do next. We recognise that we sometimes get things wrong, but we are kind to ourselves when we do, understanding that we were just doing our best and that life isn't neat-and-tidy and packaged up in a way that we can make black-and-white 'right or wrong' decisions all of the time. Rob Nairn calls this modelling the "compassionate mess".

Although it may seem obvious, it's really worth reminding

ourselves that the point-of-view of another person is equally as important and valid as our own, irrespective of age or any other variable. We may remember from our own childhood how frustrating it can feel if we feel our lives are being controlled by someone else and that this is the almost perpetual experience of most children, particularly so in our current school environments. But each of us, including children, is the expert in how we feel – unless we can walk in the shoes of another we can never truly know what their experience is and how they feel. As adults, we may or may not know best in any situation. We may as adults have a greater ability to view a situation from the perspective of the bigger picture (for example, your child may be desperate to jump in puddles whilst wearing their new shoes, but you as the adult may realise that the shoes will not have time to dry before that visit to Auntie Jean and those poor little feet will be very unwilling to stay in wet shoes all day); however, asking a child to comply with our request without an explanation and without any empathy for their feelings will often lead to defiance, or ignorant compliance. Often parents say to me that they just wish their child would do what they say without asking questions all the time! I tend to reply that actually it's great news if their child is questioning and sometimes resistant – studies have shown that children who aren't inclined to follow orders blindly tend to be more successful in life. As we develop our willingness to be a compassionate mess, we learn the strength in expressing vulnerability (and so does our child), and we deal with each situation in a dance of honouring both practicalities and feelings.

Here is an exercise that works with the intention of healing our inner child – something that each of us must do on our journey towards greater balance.

18.1 Exercise: Inner Child Healing*

Get a picture of yourself as a child – an innocent version of you. If you notice that the picture you've chosen doesn't represent an 'innocent' or 'untainted' version of you, then it may be helpful to see if you can find a younger picture of yourself, at a time when you do see yourself as having been completely innocent. Surround the chosen picture with crystals, candles or petals or anything else that feels appropriate. This exercise may feel a little tender. Please approach the practice with curiosity and gentleness, and note that we're not trying to force anything in particular to happen. If at any point any feelings arising feel too much, then perhaps you could either take yourself to a safe place in your mind, or alternatively let go of any visualisation and come back to the sensations of the breath. As with all of the practices, it's not possible to 'get it wrong' – your experience, whatever it is, is the practice.

Sitting quietly and with your eyes closed (if that feels OK), allowing the face to soften. Beginning to tune in to the sensations of the breath; perhaps this is the first time that you've noticed your breath today. Focus on your breathing for a while, seeing if you can experience each breath as if for the first time, allowing each in-breath to be a new beginning and each out-breath a complete letting go.

Take some time to get in touch with the sensations of the breath as it moves through the body, noticing where the physical sensations are strongest for you in relation to the breath. For some it's the chest, for others the nostrils, and for others the belly. Perhaps for you it's one of these places, or maybe it's somewhere different, like the shoulders or the back.

Following just this breath, in this moment.

And now bringing to mind a compassionate being – visualising the soft, loving expression on their face, their complete acceptance of you just as you are. They see the difficulties that you face and have such tender-hearted compassion towards your suffering.

Set the intention to allow the flow of loving-kindness from their heart to yours as a physical sensation. Can you tune into it? How does it feel? What physical sensations are here? Maybe there's numbness or a sense of resistance or closing down – if so, that's OK, nothing wrong. If you're not aware of any sensation then that's also fine, just noticing that. There's no wrong way to feel.

Then visualising or having a felt sense of a younger version of yourself sitting in front of you, and noticing any reaction within the body, any change in physical sensations.

Visualise or intend to have a felt sense of loving-kindness being sent from your heart towards the heart of the younger you, perhaps even visualising the younger you being surrounded by this love, and tune into any physical sensations that present themselves as you do that. Is there an emotion or a mixture of emotions that arises? Any thoughts? Maybe there's a sense of numbness, or resistance – again, nothing wrong with that, just noticing. Is it possible to hold this younger version of you in a really tender-hearted space, aware of the challenges that this younger version of you has faced as they moved through life? Is it possible to forgive yourself for the 'mistakes' of the past, accepting that your actions were a result of your level of conscious awareness at the time; in other words, you were simply doing your best and finding your way, just as we all do.

Not getting involved with and carried away by any sensations, emotions or thoughts that arise, but just noticing them, curiously, patiently, allowing whatever is present to be just as it is, as best you can.

Finishing the practice by bowing (metaphorically speaking) to your own fierce courage and thanking yourself for being willing to shine a light into those dark corners.

Remind yourself that your purpose in *each moment* with your child is to be present, to allow presence, i.e. conscious awareness, to flow into the moment. When we can do this then there's a power and a radiance that infuses the moment with possibilities – for connection, for growth, and for shifts in perception (miracles) to occur. There will be oh so many 'unconscious' moments when we meet a difficulty with our child, so we can start small in training ourselves to be present for the little things so that we are more likely to be able to stay present in the midst of something big.

For example, my eldest child will often drop his dirty socks right next to his laundry basket, as if the extra step to make it to the laundry basket is just one step too far! These are the perfect little moments to practise bringing presence to the moment. As I notice the socks lying on the floor then there's a strong pull towards 'unconscious' behaviour; I might find myself starting to huff and puff, and my mind may start to engage in stories of how this is completely unfair and how I'll deal with him when he gets home from school. My mind hops between the past (thinking of how many times he's done this before) and the future (predicting the conversation we'll have and the attitude he may well have) and I get angrier by the minute! Does this sound familiar? And yet there's a different way for things to go here. I can notice the socks on the floor and notice the sudden activity in my mind. I can notice the thoughts but let them go, and bring my attention to my breathing, curious about the movement of breath through my body in this moment. I can feel my feet on the floor and notice the small knots of tension that have crept into my stomach and my shoulders. I can invite those areas to soften, and I can breathe more deeply for a few breaths. I can then choose whether to lift the socks myself or whether to communicate to my son, upon his return from school, my need for this dirty laundry to be placed in his laundry basket for reasons of hygiene and to avoid making extra work for me. If I choose the latter, then it's important that I communicate my need without specific attachment to the result. I must be willing to hear and be open to my son's needs and be willing to compromise based on what I hear. If I ask him to pick up the socks "or else" then I will have achieved what I wanted through exerting a need for control rather than a genuine wish for each of our needs to be met through communication. The conversation might go a little like this:

ME: "Darling, could I talk to you for a moment about your room?"

SON: "Ugh, do I have to?"

ME: (showing willingness to compromise) "Well, not precisely at this moment if you're in the middle of something. I can come back in a bit if that would be better?"

SON: "No, I guess it's OK. I can talk now."

ME: (being specific rather than general) "Great. So I noticed that your dirty socks didn't quite make it to your laundry basket and wanted to make you aware that it's been 3 times this week that this has happened. Would you be willing to make more effort to put them into your laundry basket please?"

SON: "Muuuuuuuuum, what's the big deal? I just throw them over there and sometimes they don't make it! I should be able to have my room how I want it."

ME: "Well I guess that dirty socks on the floor probably doesn't feel like much of an issue to you, perhaps because you're not too concerned about cleanliness. Your room is *untidy* because it's your space and you choose to have it that way, but we've discussed previously why *unclean* isn't really an option because I feel concerned about health implications. Having smelly socks on the floor makes your carpet smell and is not hygienic. I have a need for our home to be a clean and healthy environment for everyone."

SON: "Well, I just don't have the same need, Mum!"

ME: "I do understand that, darling, and I was pretty messy

myself when I was your age, but your choice in this particular matter affects other people, and makes more work for me if I have to pick your socks up. It feels pretty hard doing all of the tasks that I have to do each day to look after all of you such as cooking, cleaning and laundry, and sometimes I feel a bit overwhelmed. I felt that way earlier today and so I wanted to talk to you about it. I would so appreciate your help with this. Would you be willing to make more effort in putting your dirty laundry into the basket?"

SON: "Well, if it's a big deal for you then OK. I hadn't realised you feel overwhelmed sometimes – I don't want you to feel like that."

ME: "Thank you for saying that, darling. I think everyone feels a little overwhelmed sometimes and it's not just because of you and your stinky socks (big grin) but if you can help in the household by taking care of small things like your socks then it can make such a difference as I can't run the house on my own. We're a team! <pause> I love you, darling."

SON: "Love you too, Mum (grin). Can you go away now please?!"

On the whole, we completely underestimate the powerful effect that our choice of language has on those on the receiving end of it. Things can go very differently if we're caught up in the stories of the mind and in reactivity. Noticing the dirty socks on the floor, we might be seething with rage by the time the offender returns home from school, and say something like, "This is disgusting! Sort yourself out! How many times do I have to tell you? You're going to run me into an early grave if I have to keep picking up after you." And the child is quite likely to hear, "*You're* disgusting! There's something wrong with you! Your behaviour is making me ill." Choosing our words more carefully, we are careful to avoid blaming anyone else for how we feel because we are aware that we have a *choice* about how we relate to our experience and that our thoughts are not facts, they are simply electrical impulses moving through us. Practising mindfulness enables us to step into the eye of the storm and to see the storm for what it is; a recognition is there that we are not the storm and that the storm will pass.

Case Study: Yvonne (mother)

Just wanted to share some happiness with you. My little one was having a full-blown tantrum today, screaming to the point of coughing. I used your BE.LOVE and it totally transformed the situation. When usually I would have been in tears of embarrassment and rushing to get home, I was able to just be unfazed by the starers and focus solely on my little child in distress and focus on what I could do for her (and not on what I could do to stop the starers). I felt completely in control and not my usual flustered mess. You have no idea how much this method has helped me. I'm so grateful you created it!

Inspired by Naomi Aldort's tool (known as 'SALVE') for dealing with difficult parenting moments and also the 'RAIN' practice taught by many mindfulness teachers, I developed the 'BE.LOVE' method for bringing open-hearted awareness to a moment of difficulty. The steps are as follows:

B – Breathe – bring your attention to your breath for a moment or two. Is your breathing slow or fast, deep or shallow, ragged or even? Take a couple of deeper breaths and then allow the breath to settle back to its natural rhythm.

E – Enquire – what story am I telling myself right now? Does it involve a 'should' or 'shouldn't'? Bring your full attention to this situation and pay close attention to what is actually going on here in your body and in your mind. In particular, pay attention to any default 'program' (or habitual way of responding) that you're running in your mind – be aware that your reaction in this situation may be driven by behaviours of your own parent(s) that you're unconsciously copying.

. **(Pause)** – So much more than just physically coming into stillness. In this pause there is space, if we choose to drop into it. Notice, if you can, the pause between the in-breath and the out-breath, and the pause between the out-breath and the in-breath. Notice how the space supports the form of the breath. There is far more space between the atoms that comprise our body than there is matter. Each atom is absolutely tiny compared to the space between each atom, and so the body is actually mostly space, it just looks (and usually feels!) very solid and dense. If we choose to tap into a sense of space in this moment, then we are no longer locked into the past. In the space of the present moment there are infinite possibilities, and we are not bound by habitual ways of reacting – we can choose to rewrite the software program that's running in the mind and choose a different output, a different way. Same trigger, different response.

L – Listen carefully, deeply and attentively. Feel your feet on the floor as you listen. Listen carefully to what your child is *actually* saying to you – their communication of what they need in this situation will come from many cues including the tone of what they're saying and their body language, not just their words.

O – Open your heart – direct your attention to your chest area and intend for that area to be 'activated' so that you listen and act with and from your heart rather than your head.

V – Validate your child's feelings. As best as you can, show the child that you understand what they are communicating and feeling, and embody a deep respect for their feelings and an acceptance of whatever their feelings are. Convey a sense that *all* feelings are OK to have – none are rejected.

E – Empower – offer choices, after all, we want to raise children who can make decisions for themselves and explore how things work out. Pause before you say, "No!" Listen to your child's feelings and needs, communicate your own feelings and needs and then empower the child by enabling them to make choices. Treat the child as you wish to be treated yourself.

I have used the BE.LOVE method many times with my own children, and taught it to many parents who have found it extremely helpful (when they can remember to employ it!). One parent who attended one of my mindful parenting workshops found the method so helpful that she had a little bumblebee next to a heart with a dot in-between tattooed on to her arm so that she wouldn't forget!

I have a wonderfully vivid memory of the method in action one evening when my youngest son, who had recently turned four, did not want me to brush his teeth before going to bed. It was important for me that his teeth were clean before he went to sleep. The situation turned into a bit of a battle, with his little face going redder and redder and him starting to stomp up and down with anger, and me raising my voice and also getting angrier and angrier. I was very tired, and so was he. After a minute or so, my mind alerted me to the fact that I was not being mindful. I *was* the storm. I stopped and became aware that my breathing was fast and shallow. I noticed the knot of tension in my stomach, the glowing heat coming from my face, the story of "but I'm tired and he should just go to bed easily like he always does" running through my mind. I looked at my red-faced little child, bent down, held his hand lightly, and said, "I'm thinking that maybe you're feeling angry just now, because you don't want me to brush your teeth?" A tearful nod. "OK, I can understand that. Can you show me where you're feeling the anger in your body?" He gestured swiftly to his head and his stomach. "Fantastic that you've noticed that, darling. And does the anger have a shape, and a colour?" He grumpily replied that it was bright red and very spikey! "Ah, OK, thank you for telling me that, and that's great noticing. I'm hoping that you can understand how important it is to me that we clean your teeth before you go to bed so that your teeth stay nice and healthy. Would you like to climb up on the step next to the sink and I could show you how to brush your teeth yourself? Perhaps I could help you a little bit, but I can see you're getting a bigger boy now and you'd like to do more things for yourself." A tearful nod and the storm had abated.

On another occasion, Logan came out of bed one evening and said he was missing Daddy. My logical mind immediately thought, "But you'll see Daddy tomorrow, that's not long to wait," however, I noticed the thought and realised it wasn't very helpful to my child in this moment. With an awareness of the flow of my breath and sensations of heaviness in my own chest as I observed the tears in his eyes, I bent down to him and asked him where in his body he was feeling this feeling of missing his daddy – could he find the place? He nodded and pointed to his tummy, to his throat and to his eyes. I asked him to see if he could bring kindness to these parts of his body and he asked how. I noticed he had 'Buchan' in his hand – his cuddly blanket that he's had since he was 6 weeks old – I asked him if he would like to place Buchan softly over his tummy with the intention of bringing kindness to his tummy, and to place his hands over the top of the blanket to allow the warmth from his hands to also bring kindness to his tummy, and then to do the same for other parts of his body. He tried it for a few seconds and then nodded and headed off back to bed. A few moments to really feel what he was feeling, and to feel heard, was all that he had needed.

19

Working with Groups

I've come to a frightening conclusion that I am the decisive element in the classroom. It's my personal approach that creates the climate. It's my daily mood that makes the weather. As a teacher, I possess a tremendous power to make a child's life miserable or joyous. I can be a tool of torture or an instrument of inspiration. I can humiliate or heal. In all situations, it is my response that decides whether a crisis will be escalated or de-escalated and a child humanized or dehumanized.
Haim G. Ginott

Children and adolescents really embrace mindfulness when we make the learning invitational, but we have to do things a little differently than we would if teaching a group of adults. For one, the group we're working with may not have chosen to learn mindfulness – it might be something you or the school you work in has decided to introduce to a class. Particularly in a group of conscripts, there will most likely be those who will (at least initially) be closed to what mindfulness can bring to their lives. As facilitators we must do all that we can to ensure that those who *do* sense the potential value of mindfulness are not prevented from experiencing each session as fully as they may wish to by those who may be more interested in being disruptive. At the same time, we wish to maintain a sense of space and allowing, and a feeling that mindfulness classes are very different to other academic subjects.

You may be starting to get the picture that there's quite a lot to juggle when we facilitate mindfulness with a group; as well as a depth of knowledge on the subject matter that is the teaching material for the classes, it also requires the ability to really 'walk the talk' of holding a full-faceted awareness of what is going on, both externally and internally, constantly monitoring:

- what is going on for you – maintaining grounded awareness,
- how the group is as a whole,
- how individuals are relating to each other,
- what the individual needs of the participants may be,
- the environment (temperature, safety, noise etc.), and
- the pacing of the session, keeping an eye on time.

Leading a group of children in a meditation, at least at the start of working with the group, can sometimes feel rather like herding jellyfish and is where we really require the foundation of a strong mindfulness practice for ourselves so that we can model an 'OKness' with whatever is thrown at us! With younger children, i.e. of nursery or primary school age, the slippery jellyfish can take the form of fidgeting, poking each other, crawling around the floor, silly noises etc. With older children, the difficulty with focusing attention and novelty of learning something so different as contemplative practice can lead to fidgeting, distracting each other and generally quite excitable energy. In such situations, my best advice is to have a strong mindfulness practice in place so that your own practice of facing difficulties with curiosity and kindness will carry you through whatever transpires, and (just as importantly) *keep your sense of humour!* Without humour, all is lost, well perhaps not all, but really if we can't see the hilarity of our human predicaments then we probably shouldn't be trying to teach mindfulness to a group of children!

Teaching mindfulness to children is not for the faint-hearted but it *is* for the light-hearted and it should be fun. Indeed, every opportunity for light-heartedness and fun should be embraced. Life can be fun, spontaneous, playful, joyful. Too often it is serious, full of responsibility and heavy. Sometimes in secondary schools a little too much weight is placed on the shoulders of each pupil when they are told to study their hardest to achieve the best grades possible in exams, or else they'll be stuck in a dead-end job for the rest of their lives. Whilst of course we want pupils to feel motivated to do their best, the thought that, "You'd better do well or else you're dooming yourself to a life of misery" is an extremely unhelpful one to implant in anyone's mind, and quite untrue! How fortunate that I chose not to believe that I had to adhere to any one particular path once I had chosen it, otherwise I'd be a very unhappy software engineer right now!

If you're working with groups in a school setting, then I can't recommend Amy Saltzman's *A Still Quiet Place* book highly enough – it's primarily aimed at teaching within schools and is beautifully written. Susan Kaiser Greenland's *The Mindful Child* book is also very rich in content for those working with groups of children and full of lovely ideas.

Really the purpose of any of these types of books is to help inspire you to get creative yourself. Learn what works for you in your own practice and then find creative ways to share what you have learned with the age group you're working with. Your own practice will lead you down avenues of creativity that you never even dreamed of! For example, you may find yourself in the bath paying close attention to the bubbles of the bubble bath, noticing how the light is reflected by the smooth and shiny surface of each bubble. You may find yourself noticing with each breath in and out that more and more of the little bubbles pop and disappear. It may suddenly occur to you that children love bubbles, and the primary one class that you're teaching would love to gather around some washing-up bowls filled with a little warm water and lots of bubbles and pretend that they're popping the bubbles with each in-breath and each out-breath. What actually transpires of course is an awareness of the breath in a light way and a focusing of the mind on the present moment – perfect!

Practicalities and Holding Space

If you're leading a group in a lying down meditation and it's a mixed class (as Richard Burnett of the Mindfulness in Schools Project wisely suggests), it's a good idea to ensure that legs are directed towards the wall so that boys don't try to look up girls' skirts, and it's helpful to give some guidance around personal space, inviting each pupil to find a space that's their own and to ensure that even if they feel very distracted, they respect the space of those around them and don't deliberately try to distract anyone else. In fact, the 'respecting space' isn't just relevant to lying down meditations, it's important much more generally – it's really helpful to encourage the children to be in their own space both physically and mentally during each practice and to allow each member of the group to have their own experience.

Before beginning to work with a group of children or adolescents it can really set the tone for a collaborative way of working if you invite the group (with your help) to come up with ground rules for practice, perhaps getting the group to work together in smaller groups of twos or threes to write a list of the things that they feel they need in order to feel safe and to have their space and time respected. These lists can then be collated to form a ground rules document that every group member is aware of and can feel supported by (in conjunction with you holding the space for them in the light of their chosen ground rules) during your practice time together. So if, for example, the group identifies that they would like no one else to talk when someone is speaking, then as the facilitator if someone starts to talk over someone else you can direct their attention to the ground rules and you may choose to say something along the lines of, "I'm noticing that you're keen to speak and I'm very interested in hearing your contribution, but I'd like to draw your attention to the ground rules and highlight that the group has chosen to give space to each person who wishes to speak, and so I'm going to ask you to hold on to what you have to say for a few moments until <insert

name> has finished speaking."

As the facilitator, it's your job to 'hold the space'; that means ensuring that your time together as a group feels safe for each group and making sure that one group member doesn't prevent another group member from benefiting from the experience whilst being as allowing and accepting as possible. Sound a little tricky? Well, yes, it is. It's also potentially one of the most rewarding experiences that you may ever have.

Environment

If you're a school teacher intending to teach meditation to children with whom you already work academically, then it is very useful to use cues such as a change in lighting and a change in your body position in order to signal the change from *doing* mode to *being* mode to the students. For example, if you normally stand up and pace across the front of the class when you teach, perhaps you could consider bringing your chair from behind your desk and sit facing the students. If you have a breakout room or access to floor cushions, then it might be enjoyable for the students to experience their meditation time as 'special', but mindfulness meditation and visualisation can be practised absolutely anywhere so please don't feel that you need to acquire any special props or have access to a quiet, tranquil environment before you can introduce mindfulness into your school. The Mindfulness in Schools Project's curricula are in general taught to primary and secondary school pupils in their normal classrooms, with pupils sitting at their desks and with all of the normal school disruptions such as noisy bells, knocks on the door and noise travelling from hallways and next-door class-rooms.

At first you may find that pupils are quite distracted when you are leading practices, with their attention very easily diverted from whatever you may be asking them to pay attention to, but little-by-little (and sometimes much more quickly than you expect) you will start to notice differences in ability to focus. One of the biggest factors fostering this change is your own behaviour. If you model jumpiness, distractedness or frustration when the classroom is interrupted, then this is what the pupils will reflect back to you. If, however, you model a complete acceptance and non-reaction to interruptions such as unexpected noises (except those that require your immediate attention such as another teacher asking for your help) then the pupils will learn by your example.

Motivation

Just as we re-energise our motivation at the start of each formal practice, it's really helpful each time we work with a group to touch in once again with the reasons behind what we're doing. Our motivation will carry us through a really tricky session where the children all seemed very fidgety and distracted and chaos ensued after one of the kids passed wind so loudly during one of the practices that another of the kids fell off his chair because he was laughing so hard. These are the moments when we will ask ourselves why we thought it was a good idea to teach mindfulness to a group of young people, and these are the moments when we may keep ourselves on course by reminding ourselves that what drives us, at some core level, is a heartfelt wish to make the world a better place. We are aware of how much mindfulness has changed our own lives in a positive way, and wish to share that with others. Keeping sight of our motivation can also freshen and enliven our teaching.

Tibetan Buddhist nun, Pema Chödrön, in her book *When Things Fall Apart* eloquently sums up the path we set ourselves when we embark on the journey of mindfulness by telling us that it's really about *learning to relax in the midst of chaos* and not to panic. Nowhere is this truer than when we facilitate mindfulness in a group setting, quite literally learning to relax in the midst of the chaos, not knowing what each moment might bring but trusting that whatever emerges will be OK – this is the path of spiritual growth. The lessons we will learn through the situations we will face may at times feel painful and even humbling, so our motivation must be strong and so must our compassionate inner resources – this will give us the strength to turn towards our difficulties and not give up.

Flexibility

You will need to decide what material you are going to deliver to your group. If you're a school teacher and you feel that your own practice is well established, you may decide to use some material from books such as this one and plan the sessions yourself; alternatively you may decide to learn to deliver a set curriculum such as the Mindfulness in Schools Project '.b' or 'Paws b'. You may choose to engage with the Connected Kids™ training or similar, if you wish to learn to work more creatively and without a set curriculum. If you do decide to deliver a curriculum, then be aware that there is a delicate balance between covering the relevant part of a curriculum within a session whilst also being open and responsive to what is arising within the group, and so you will need to have good organisational and time-management skills, and an in-depth knowledge of the curriculum along with a willingness to be flexible. Mindfulness facilitators in general need to be extremely flexible, always supporting the needs of the group as far as possible and balancing the teaching points for the session with the natural arising of material within the group that space needs to be allowed for; there are, however, additional needs for flexibility when working with children and young people – groups of children and young people can be far more diverse in terms of their behaviour than groups of adults. In addition, we're often limited to short lesson durations and limited classroom space, meaning that we have to adapt the practice to whatever we have to work with in terms of the venue.

Relating to the Group Members

Often as adults we have lost touch with how it is to be a child or young person, and often our own childhood has been very different to the kind of childhood that young people today experience, and so it can be harder to relate on a personal level to young participants. Our mindfulness and compassion, however, keep us alert to, and aware of, the universal nature of human suffering, and this combined with a sense of playfulness, openness and a commitment to nurturing our inner child can really help us see our struggles in life as essentially the same – we all wish to be healthy, we all wish to be happy, we all wish to feel safe, and we all wish that life will go easily for us. Key in relating to the group members is an honesty with ourselves and the group, being in touch with our feelings, and bringing warmth, confidence and compassion to ourselves and our experience.

If we experience challenging group members then it's really helpful to see if we can extend the sentiment of Rumi's Guest House poem to our external world, and see those challenging group members as being there to teach us valuable lessons. Staying present with compassion for ourselves and these 'difficult' group members will help us to transform our relationship with whatever it is that we see, but don't like.

Embodiment of mindfulness

Several research studies have strongly pointed to the 'person of the teacher' (that is everything that the teacher embodies) as being absolutely central to the teaching, rather than a passing on of intellectual knowledge. When working with young people, it has become deeply apparent to me that the relationship must be built on trust and authenticity, or 'the game's a bogey' as they say. Embodiment is not something that we can learn as mindfulness facilitators – it is a direct result of our mindfulness practice – which is why it is so important to *intend* to have a well-established daily mindfulness practice even if you feel your practice is a little higgledy-piggledy at present.

Guiding group practices

Guiding mindfulness practices requires a knowledge of the elements of the practices along with a skilful use of language to guide participants in their experience in an open, invitational, curious and friendly way, conveying a sense of spaciousness and room for whatever is there to be there. It is also necessary to be very sensitive to what may be arising for participants. The Body Scan, in particular, can sometimes bring to light some difficulties or traumas so we must guide the practice whilst experiencing it ourselves so that we can lead from a place of authenticity but also keeping a portion of our attention on the participants to monitor how they are.

Often when leading a practice from a place of experiencing it quite deeply ourselves, we find that the natural tendency is for the voice to become very relaxed and the volume drops. It's helpful to bear this in mind and try to ensure that your voice can be heard by everyone in the room throughout the practice.

Inquiry

Inquiry as it relates to the facilitation of mindfulness is often referred to as 'investigative dialogue', 'inquiry process', 'interactive inquiry' or 'insight dialogue'. You've already experienced the role of inquiry after a practice through snippets of dialogue at the end of some of the practices earlier in the book and you may have noticed that these have been short and light in the examples I've given. There's quite a strong emphasis on inquiry in adult mindfulness courses, and it's rather like a mutual dance of almost meditative conversation between the facilitator and inquiree, where the facilitator holds a space of present-moment awareness, friendliness and curiosity in order to tease out the various facets of the inquiree's experience with sensitivity and humility. The inquiree's mind will tend to drift off on to various trains of thought and it is the role of the facilitator to gently redirect the inquiree's attention to the felt sense of their experience. This process of teasing out the facets of experience tends to bring a fresh perspective – a different way of looking at the experience; a shift in perception. It is much harder to bring about this shift in perception by ourselves – particularly at the beginning of our mindfulness training we are easily distracted and tend to drift off on trains of thought which take us away from this moment and away from the felt sense within the body.

My experience of working with children and teens, and this is very much in line with Susan Kaiser Greenland's feeling about inquiry in *The Mindful Child*, tells me that we need to tread very carefully with inquiry after practices when we're working with groups of young people. Teens spend much of their time flipping between very much wanting to be seen (cue brightly dyed hair) and very much wanting to be invisible (cue shrinking body language in the corner of a classroom), and singling out group members can feel agonising for those wishing to be invisible. I find it helpful to use a mixture of closed and open questions during inquiry. Those who are wishing to be less visible may shake their head or nod in response to a closed question, and those who are chattier will use the open questions to volunteer a bit more of their experience. There have been many times for me when it has felt like tumbleweed was blowing through the classroom, such was the complete silence for an interminable length of time after I've asked a question. These are the moments when we practise patience and trust, and model acceptance and allowing as best we can! If all else fails, and nobody speaks even after you've patiently asked several different questions and left lots of time for responses, you may choose to volunteer something of your own experience and then see if anyone else had a similar experience. If you do tell of your own experience, then keep it light – don't volunteer a deeply personal moment of insight that may make group members feel uncomfortable, for example the moment when you realised that you were holding expectations for your partner in line with the expectations you had of your parent!

Keep inquiry to quite simple questions, such as:

- How was that practice for you? What did you notice?
- Was there somewhere in the body that you could feel that?
- What did it feel like – can you describe it?
- Thank you for sharing that. Isn't it interesting to watch what the mind does?! Did anyone have a similar experience or a different experience that they'd like to share?

When facilitating learning in mindfulness we don't have a set of established goals or concrete learning outcomes that we judge the 'success' or 'failure' of the participants' learning by; as facilitators we meet the participants where they're at, and the journey for each of us when learning mindfulness is a very personal and quite unique one. Although experience is indeed unique, we often journey through life thinking that our habitual patterns, worries, fears and anxieties are particular and peculiar to us, and considerable relief and comfort comes from the knowledge that we are not alone in these and that other people feel the same way. Perhaps much of the benefit of delivering mindfulness to groups is the 'normalization' of each individual experience; experience that is brought to light through the inquiry process. If there's one very useful thing to come out of inquiry with children and teens, perhaps it is this – helping each member of the group to no longer see themselves as alone in their difficulties. Having a sense of common humanity, i.e. shared human experience, is a powerful antidote to the isolation that can so commonly lead to depression. We really are all in this together. All of us have minds that are very unruly and have very unhelpful tendencies.

All of us have emotional systems that overwhelm rational thought and this is not necessarily a bad thing, but we're not usually taught how to work skilfully with what we have. Helping a young person to realise that they're not alone and there's nothing wrong with them is, for me, the most rewarding thing that I could do with my time. Ever.

Creating a Compassionate Classroom

Rather than seeing mindfulness and compassion as additional subjects that can be taught in a classroom, maybe by now we can see the sense in bringing them to the heart of everything that goes on in the classroom. Here are just a few ideas for creating a mindful and compassionate classroom – I hope they inspire you to get creative:

- Support the kids in running their own lunchtime practice sessions. Encourage the children to lead each other in short practices such as MOP, breath awareness, heart breathing etc.
- Use sticky dots as mentioned in Chapter 17, for example in a classroom you may wish to put a red dot on the outside and inside of the door to remind children to come back to the present moment as they enter and as they leave, or pink (or green) dots on their jotters to remind them to be present and to bring kindness to any difficulties they experience.
- Have a 'kind wishes' box somewhere in the classroom and encourage students to write a name on a scrap piece of paper and post it in the box whenever they wish to recognise that someone's having a hard time. Great if they want to post their own name – actively support this.
- Celebrate acts of compassion by asking students to place a small stone in the 'compassion jar' each time they notice a compassionate act (either by themselves or by someone else) – it could be a simple act such as someone holding a

door open for a student who's struggling with a pile of books. This will help students to be more aware of the little acts of compassion that are happening all around them and more likely to act compassionately themselves.

A Primary Teacher's Perspective

Learning to teach meditation to children seemed the natural next step after I discovered the benefits of meditation for myself. As a teacher, I could see immediately how the techniques I had learned could help my pupils and improve the ethos of my classroom. The first stage of my training to teach children meditation (Connected Kids Level 1) was brilliant! I loved it and it filled me with such enthusiasm about how meditation and mindful activities could help my pupils – helping both sides of the brain to work together, reducing anxiety and increasing self-esteem to name a few reasons. I was slightly apprehensive but excited to try some of the meditations and activities with my class. My head teacher was happy for me to use the techniques in my classroom which was great and she has always been supportive, arranging time for me to go into other classes and share what I had learned with the other staff.

I wondered if meditating in the classroom with 25 pupils would be difficult but it really hasn't been at all. Before I begin I always make sure my classroom doesn't feel cluttered and I imagine a pink flame in the centre of the classroom, inviting any negative energy to go into the flame. The children close the blinds and turn of the lights and find a space where they are comfortable (I let them choose whether they lie/sit on the floor/sit on their chair). Initially I found the breathing and body scan meditations the easiest as they are less personal and the children enjoyed them. I did a few guided visualisation meditations with them (mainly following a script to begin with) and these instantly became their favourite. Twenty-five children may seem like a large number of children to meditate with and you can't personalise the meditations as much but I know my children well and have found as my confidence has developed I have been able to use my instincts to lead meditations that suit the needs of the class.

Since further consolidating my training I have been able to lead each class in the school in a few meditations and found I was able to adapt the meditations to suit the age group of each class. Each teacher took part in the meditations with their class. The primary 1/2 teacher loves it and says it has had a massive impact on her class. The pupils are much calmer and able to concentrate more easily. Her pupils draw/write about their experiences, the pictures they have drawn are beautiful and they are accompanied with phrases such as "I was so happy", "my door was so nice", "I love it – it was amazing" and "secret place for me, so happy".

My pupils regularly request 'relaxation time' and the positive effects are definitely noticeable. My main learning intentions have been to encourage self-acceptance, loving-kindness towards self and others and an ability to let go and recognise that thoughts aren't facts. I am pleased to see the impact of this in my classroom every day. It is now just part of what we do at school.

Jenny, Primary School Teacher

20

In Awe and Wonder – a final message

And then all that has divided us will merge.
And then compassion will be wedded to power
And then softness will come to a world that is harsh and unkind.
And then both men and women will be gentle.
And then both women and men will be strong.
And then no person will be subject to another's will.
And then all will be rich and free and varied.
And then the greed of some will give way to the needs of many.
And then all will share equally in the earth's abundance.
And then all will care for the sick and the weak and the old.
And then all will nourish the young.
And then all will cherish life's creatures.
And then all will live in harmony with each other and the earth.
And then everywhere will be called Eden once again.

Judy Chicago

Our journey together through the pages of this book now comes to an end, but I hope you will choose to join me at www.facebook.com/groups/AwakeningChild to connect and receive ongoing support. I would absolutely love to hear about your experiences with the practices and others may also really benefit from what you share.

Key to this continual process of awakening both ourselves and our child to *all that we can be* is a commitment to keeping up our own practice because the outer world reflects our inner world. If our inner weather pattern is stormy then our outer situation in both our home and work lives will reflect this.

If, as a parent or teacher, you realise you got it wrong, it wasn't a mistake. Congratulate yourself that you noticed you'd choose to do things differently next time and meditate on the lessons to be learned from what happened. Indeed, *be willing* to get it wrong and to move through the journey of life being a compassionate mess – it's much less stressful than trying to model compassionate perfection!

20.1 Exercise: A Final Reflection

Wherever you are this moment, intend to move into Weeble mode, finding the breath in the body and feeling the weight of the body as it rests. Spend some time with each of the questions that follow, dropping in each question to the quiet lake of the mind and see if anything bubbles up in response, rather than analysing and looking for answers.

What's your experience in this moment? How are you feeling, as you find yourself close to the end of the book?

What messages, if any, will you take away from these pages?

Do you feel different now from how you felt when you first opened the book? If so, what has changed?

If it would feel nurturing to do so, place a hand over the centre of your chest and finish your reflection by honouring yourself for all that you are, and all that you will awaken in a child, or perhaps in many children. You. Are. Amazing.

I hope that you feel empowered to bring mindfulness into your household or working life in a way that feels right for you and those around you. I bow to you and your brave soul, and am so deeply grateful that you have chosen to walk with me awhile by reading this book. Each of us committing to change this world for our children brings more light to the darkness, and we create ripples of change that are causing a momentum-gathering shift. Soon this will (and must for our survival) reach critical mass so that return to our old way of being in conflict with each other is not possible. We create a new world, one where the heart guides us rather than the head. Your open-hearted courage to do the inner work necessary to fuel this evolution of humankind fills me with awe, wonder and hope. Thank you, dearest you.

Appendix A – Resources for Adults

Mindfulness and Compassion for Adults

Brach, T., 2003. *Radical Acceptance: Awakening the Love that Heals Fear and Shame Within Us.* London: Rider.

Chödrön, P., 2012. *Living Beautifully.* Shambhala Publications.

Chödrön, P., 1997. *When Things Fall Apart.* 2005 edition. US: Shambhala Publications.

Claxton, G., 1997. *Hare Brain, Tortoise Mind: Why Intelligence Increases When You Think Less.* 1998 edition. London: Fourth Estate.

Gilbert, P. and Choden, 2013. *Mindful Compassion.* London: Constable & Robinson Ltd.

Kabat-Zinn, J., 1994. *Wherever You Go, There You Are: Mindfulness Meditation for Everyday Life.* New York: Hyperion.

Kabat-Zinn, J., 1990. *Full Catastrophe Living: Using the Wisdom of Your Body and Mind to Face Stress, Pain and Illness.* Fifteenth Anniversary Definition edition. New York: Bantam Dell.

Nairn, R., 2010. *Diamond Mind: A Psychology of Meditation.* 2nd edition. South Africa: Kairon Press.

Tsoknyi Rinpoche and Swanson, E., 2012. *Open Heart, Open Mind: A Guide to Inner Transformation.* London: Rider.

Psychology

Begley, S. and Davidson, R., 2012. *The Emotional Life of Your Brain.* London: Hodder & Stoughton.

Siegel, D. and Bryson, TP, 2012. *The Whole-Brain Child.* Kindle edition. London: Constable & Robinson Ltd.

Mindful Parenting

Aldort, N., 2006. *Raising Our Children, Raising Ourselves.* Bothell, WA: Book Publishers Network.

Faber, A., and Mazlish, E., 2013. *How To Talk So Kids Will Listen and Listen So Kids Will Talk*. Piccadilly Press.

Kabat-Zinn, J. and Kabat-Zinn, M., 2008. *Everyday Blessings: The Inner Work of Mindful Parenting*. New York: Hyperion.

Teaching children meditation and mindfulness

Greenland, SK, 2010. *The Mindful Child: How to Help Your Kid Manage Stress and Become Happier, Kinder, and More Compassionate*. Simon and Schuster.

Murray, L., 2012. *Calm Kids: Help Children Relax with Mindful Activities*. Floris Books.

Saltzman, A., 2014. *A Still Quiet Place: A Mindfulness Program for Teaching Children and Adolescents to Ease Stress and Difficult Emotions*. Kindle edition. New Harbinger Publications.

Snel, E., 2013. *Sitting Still Like a Frog: Mindfulness Exercises for Kids (and Their Parents)*. Shambhala Publications.

Willard, C., 2010. *Child's Mind: Mindfulness Practices to Help Our Children Be More Focused, Calm, and Relaxed*. Parallax Press.

Journaling

Braime, H., 2013. *The Ultimate Guide to Journaling*. Kindle edition.

Spirituality

Gawain, S., 2012. *Living in the Light: Follow Your Inner Guidance to Create a New Life and a New World*. 2nd edition. New World Library.

Tolle, E., 2009. *A New Earth: Create a Better Life*. Penguin.

Tolle, E., 2001. *The Power of Now: A Guide to Spiritual Enlightenment*. Yellow Kite.

Useful Websites

www.mindfulnessassociation.net

www.mindfulnet.org

http://bemindful.co.uk

Mindfulness Courses

www.mindfulnessassociation.net/MBLC.aspx

http://bemindful.co.uk/learn/find-a-course/

Online Mindfulness Courses (free)

www.mindfulnessassociation.net/Gifts.aspx

http://palousemindfulness.com/selfguidedMBSR.html

Appendix B – Resources for Children

Recorded Meditations for Younger Children
Colourful Moments by Heather Grace MacKenzie – digital download
www.cdbaby.com/cd/heathermackenzie3

Crystal Clear by Lorraine Murray – audio CD
http://www.teachchildrenmeditation.com/resources/meditations-for-teenskids/meditations-for-children/

Enchanted Meditations for Kids by Christiane Kerr – digital download
Available on Amazon.co.uk

Recorded Meditations for Teens
Wild and Precious Life by Heather Grace MacKenzie – digital download
www.cdbaby.com/cd/heathermackenzie

Mindfulness Meditations for Teens by Bodhipaksa – audio CD
Available on Amazon.co.uk

Chill Zone by Lorraine Murray – audio CD
Meditation CD for Teenage Stress
http://www.teachchildrenmeditation.com/resources/meditations-for-teenskids/meditation_cd_teenagers/

Books for Younger Children
Hayden, T., Mingyur, Y., 2009. *Ziji: The Puppy Who Learned to Meditate*. Tergar International.
The Future Teacher Foundation, 2015. *Mindfulness Colouring Book for Children*. CreateSpace Independent Publishing Platform.

Millman, D., 1991. *Secret of the Peaceful Warrior.* HJ Kramer.

Nhat Hanh, Thich, 2012. *A Handful of Quiet: Happiness in Four Pebbles.* Crds edition. Parallax Press.

Books for Older Children

Biegel, GM, 2009. *Stress Reduction Workbook for Teens: Mindfulness Skills to Help You Deal with Stress (Instant Help) (Teen Instant Help).* New Harbinger.

Ciarrochi, J., 2012. *Get Out of Your Mind and Into Your Life for Teens: A Guide to Living an Extraordinary Life (Teen Instant Help).* New Harbinger.

Vo, Dzung X., Prof., 2015. *Mindful Teen: Powerful Skills to Help You Handle Stress One Moment at a Time (Instant Help Solutions).* New Harbinger.

Willard, C., 2014. *Mindfulness for Teen Anxiety: A Workbook for Overcoming Anxiety at Home, at School, and Everywhere Else (Teen Instant Help).* New Harbinger.

Singing Bowls

www.spectrumwellbeing.co.uk/acatalog/tibetanbowls.html

Tuning Forks, Sansulas etc.

www.soundtravels.co.uk

Mandalas (free mandala printouts for colouring in)

www.printmandala.com

Sticky dots

8mm round dots – assortment of colours – www.amazon.co.uk/dp/B00NNRPJ8K

BOOKS

O is a symbol of the world, of oneness and unity; this eye represents knowledge and insight. We publish titles on general spirituality and living a spiritual life. We aim to inform and help you on your own journey in this life.

Visit our website: http://www.o-books.com

Find us on Facebook:
https://www.facebook.com/OBooks

Follow us on Twitter: @obooks

If you have enjoyed this book, why not tell other readers by posting a review on your preferred booksite? Recent bestsellers from O-Books are:

The Heart of Tantric Sex
Diana Richardson
Revealing Eastern secrets of deep love and intimacy to Western couples.
Paperback: 978-1-90381-637-0
e-book: 978-1-84694-637-0

Crystal Prescriptions: The A-Z guide to over 1,200 symptoms and their healing crystals
Judy Hall
The first in the popular series of four books, this handy little guide is packed as tight as a pill-bottle with crystal remedies for ailments.
Paperback: 978-1-90504-740-6
e-book: 978-1-84694-629-5

Take Me To Truth, Undoing the Ego
Nouk Sanchez, Tomas Vieira
The best-selling step-by-step book on shedding the Ego, using the teachings of *A Course in Miracles*.
Paperback: 978-1-84694-050-7
e-book: 978-1-84694-654-7

The 7 Myths about Love...Actually! The journey from your HEAD to the HEART of your SOUL
Mike George
Smashes all the myths about LOVE.
Paperback: 978-1-84694-288-4
e-book: 978-1-84694-682-0

The Holy Spirit's Interpretation of the New Testament:
A course in Understanding and Acceptance
Regina Dawn Akers
Following on from the strength of *A Course in Miracles*, NTI
teaches us how to experience the love and oneness of God.
Paperback: 978-1-84694-085-9
e-book: 978-1-78099-083-5

The Message of A Course In Miracles:
A translation of the Text in plain language
Elizabeth A. Cronkhite
A translation of *A Course in Miracles* into plain, everyday
language for anyone seeking inner peace. The companion
volume, *Practicing A Course in Miracles*, offers practical lessons
and mentoring.
Paperback: 978-1-84694-319-5
e-book: 978-1-84694-642-4

Rising in Love:
My Wild and Crazy Ride to Here and Now, with Amma, the
Hugging Saint
Ram Das Batchelder
Rising in Love conveys an author's extraordinary journey of
spiritual awakening with the Guru, Amma.
Paperback: 978-1-78279-687-9
e-book: 978-1-78279-686-2

The Thinker's Guide to God
Peter Vardy
An introduction to key issues in the philosophy of religion.
Paperback: 978-1-90381-622-6

Your Simple Path:
Find Happiness in every step
Ian Tucker
A guide to helping us reconnect with what is really important in our lives.
Paperback: 978-1-78279-349-6
e-book: 978-1-78279-348-9

Find more titles and sign up to our readers' newsletter at http://www.johnhuntpublishing.com/mind-body-spirit.

Follow us on Facebook at https://www.facebook.com/OBooks and Twitter at https://twitter.com/obooks.

Most titles are published in paperback and as an e-book. Paperbacks are available in physical bookshops. Both print and e-book editions are available online. Readers of e-books can click on the live links in the titles to order.